CAVALLI

CAVALLI

Jane Glover

St. Martin's Press
New York

 For information, write:
St. Martin's Press, Inc.,
175 Fifth Avenue, New York, N.Y. 10010

Printed in Great Britain

Library of Congress Catalog Card Number 77-23638

ISBN 0-312-12546-1

First published in the United States of America in 1978

Contents

Illustrations

Preface

Much of the research for this book was made possible by financial support from the Governing Body of St Hugh's College, Oxford, who awarded me a Junior Research Fellowship for two years and supplemented this with grants from the Cesaresco Martinengo fund. Some of the material in Chapters II and III has been drawn from my D.Phil. thesis, 'The Teatro Sant' Apollinare and the development of seventeenth-century Venetian opera' (Oxford, 1975).

I am profoundly grateful to all those who have offered direction and advice during the course of my research: particularly to Professor Denis Arnold and to Dr F. W. Sternfeld, who have both supplied information and infinite encouragement, and to Thomas Walker for confirming several details and for his knowledgeable comments on the manuscript of this book.

In Venice I have been assisted by the Directors and staff of the following libraries and archives: Biblioteca Marciana, Biblioteca Correr, Archivio di Stato, Casa Goldoni and Fondazione Giorgio Cini.

I would finally like to extend warmest thanks to all friends and colleagues who have made numerous miscellaneous contributions. Principal among these are Anne Ridler, with whom, as translator, I have collaborated on performing editions of Cavalli's *Rosinda, Eritrea* and *Didone*; Ellen Rosand, who has provided continuous guidance and enthusiasm; and my father, R. F. Glover, for his patient criticism of the manuscript. Others to whom gratitude is due are Lorenzo Bianconi, Jennifer Fletcher, Deborah Howard, Raymond Leppard, Auriol Milford, James Moore, Giovanni Morelli, Carlo Piastrella, my family, the BBC, Faber Music, the Wexford Festival Opera; all those who have performed in or assisted with productions of Cavalli's operas that I have edited and conducted in recent years; and indeed all who persuaded me that only wild horses would prevent me from completing this book.

CHAPTER I

Biography

In the heart of the north Italian plain, some 27 miles from Milan, lies the small but prosperous town of Crema. In 1447 it was acquired by the Venetian Republic, which was rapidly taking advantage of the death (in 1402) of its closest territorial rival, Giangaleazzo Visconti of Milan, and assuming command in most of Lombardy. Within the first half of the fifteenth century Vicenza, Verona, Padua, Brescia, Bergamo and Peschiera, along with their respective provinces, all fell to the Venetians, and the relatively small communities of Crema, Lodi and Agnadello represented the most westerly point of the empire. Apart from the years 1509 to 1512 when it was occupied by France, Crema remained under Venetian rule until the arrival of Napoleon in 1797. It was governed by a Venetian patrician with the title of 'Podestà' or 'Rettore', who had control over all matters in the town, whether civil, military or criminal. It is presumably a testimony both to the conscientious agricultural and commercial activities of Crema's people, and to the strong leadership of its successive governors, that the town remained a centre of comparative peace and prosperity for so many years.

It was here, in the parish of S. Benedetto, that Pier Francesco Caletti was born on 14 February 1602. His father, Giovanni Battista Caletti, had also been born in Crema, in 1577, and had married Victoria Bertolotti, one year his junior, on 4 May 1596.[1] Between the years 1597 and 1621 Victoria gave birth to nine children, but it appears that only three survived: they were Pier Francesco, the third to be born but the first to live, and referred to by a contemporary writer as 'primogenito',[2] Cecilia (born on 21 March 1610) and Diambra Caterina (born on 30 November 1614).[3] Francesco was baptised on the day that he was born,[4] which suggests parental anxiety as to his survival, too. But he grew up quite normally, and in his earliest years was chiefly encouraged and directed into musical activities by his father.

Little is known about Giovanni Battista Caletti, though it is clear that as an organist, teacher, composer and *maestro di cappella* at the Duomo, he was a prominent figure in this small environment. The seventeenth-century Crema historian Lodovico Canobio stated that Caletti's musical reign lasted for over 40 years, during which time he 'governed the public music of the Duomo'.[5] His only major publication, a book of madrigals, appeared in 1604.[6] The volume was dedicated to his former pupil, Angela Pallavicina,[7] and to her husband Sigismondo Trecchi, on the occasion of their wedding; and, with a business-like sense of the appropriate which perhaps foreshadowed that of his son, Caletti chose his texts with care. Among the 16 five-part madrigals is a setting of Guarini's 'Mentre vaga Angioletta', while the three pieces in eight parts, together called 'Himeneo', are specifically concerned with the wedding ('Di pargoletta e bella Angela il suono', 'Di Sigismondo il vanto' and 'Quando lieto Himeneo').

With his father's instruction and encouragement, Francesco Caletti was soon found to possess an outstanding singing voice and entered the choir of the Duomo. It was here that he first attracted the attention of current Venetian Rettore, Federico Cavalli, a conspicuously successful and popular governor. This nobleman was so impressed by the boy that, at the end of his term of office in Crema (which lasted from 3 July 1614 to 1 March 1616) he proposed to take him back to Venice and give him all the benefits of Venetian musical life. Giovanni Battista Caletti was apparently reluctant to be separated from his son (Canobio tells of the 'gran difficoltà ottenuta dal proprio padre') but was naturally honoured by the suggestion and in due course gave his consent. In the following year he was able to express his gratitude to Federico Cavalli in print. His colleague Giovanni Battista Leonetti, organist at the church of S. Agostino in Crema, published a book of five-part madrigals and dedicated them to the retiring Rettore.[8] Among the 20 pieces in the book are 'Non more, e spasmo' and a seven-part 'Balletto pastorale' by Giovanni Battista Caletti. The latter is specifically headed 'All' Illustrissimo Sig. Federico de Cavalli', and the text describes the success of his governorship:

Hor si che'l vago Aprile
Godi Crema gentile
Lieta vanne è giocosa
Che'l gran Fedrico in te risieda e posa.

This 'Balletto' may indeed be no more than the usual sycophantic eulogy of resident or retiring authority; but its apparently intentional inclusion in a printed volume of this date does suggest that Caletti intended it to be a public expression of gratitude to Federico Cavalli for the patronage accorded to his son.

* * *

It is likely that, on his arrival in Venice, the young Francesco Caletti was at least temporarily given a home by the Cavalli family, and, in courteous recognition of their extreme generosity and encouragement, he eventually adopted their name. December 1616 the boy was accepted into the choir of St. Mark's at a salary of 80 ducats per annum. Together with the castrato Felice Cazzelari from Pistoia, who was later also to enjoy operatic limelight, he sang to a selection of Procurators, and to the current *maestro di cappella*, all of whom were considerably impressed.[9] Francesco's connection with St. Mark's, which was to continue for the rest of his life, was confirmed two months later on 18 February 1617, when he was formally presented to the Doge (Giovanni Bembo).[10] His arrival could hardly have been better timed. The current *maestro di cappella* was Claudio Monteverdi, who had been appointed by the Procurators in 1612, and who was successfully restoring the standards of the Basilica's music to the level reached by his illustrious predecessors of the last century, the organists Andrea and Giovanni Gabrieli. The extent to which the young Cavalli was actually taught by Monteverdi is not clear, but their daily professional relationship at least meant that the boy acquired an essential knowledge of counterpoint which was to emerge in his own sacred compositions at various stages throughout his long life. Cavalli's talents as a keyboard player, too, soon became apparent, and on 18 May 1620 he was appointed a part-time organist at the large church of SS. Giovanni e Paolo, at an annual salalry of 30 ducats.[11] So within four years of his fortuitous arrival in Venice he had been quickly recognised as a musician of great potential talent whereby he was able to earn a comparatively comfortable living.

During the 1620's Cavalli continued to establish himself as a musician of some versatility. In 1625, Leonardo Simonetti published a collection of sacred motets for solo voice under the title *Ghirlanda Sacra*.[12] The 26 composers represented in the 45 motets included such renowned names as Monteverdi, Rovetta, Grandi, Berti and Martinengo, and among these is also the young Cavalli, described as 'Organista di SS. Giovanni e Paolo'. He continued to work at St. Mark's (in 1627 he was registered there as a tenor, although he had clearly been singing that part for some time) and he was apparently one of the many musicians employed on an *ad hoc* basis by religious confraternities for the celebrations of great festivals. In 1627 the Scuola di S. Rocco celebrated the feast of their patron saint in an extravagant style, employing a large number of musicians headed by Monteverdi, at a total cost of 1391 lire.[13] Monteverdi received 146 lire, and Cavalli, whose name appears not with players or choral singers but as a solo singer, was paid 26 lire. It is highly likely that in this same period Cavalli was employed on a similar free-lance basis by other religious institutions for their major celebrations and festivals.

But despite this acknowledged competence as a musician, it appears that these early years of Cavalli's Venetian life were not without upheaval and a certain irresponsibility. Having been wrenched from his family and his home at a comparatively early age, he virtually lost contact with Crema. The Cavalli family initially housed him, but by 1620 he was living at the house of Alvise Mocenigo,[14] which suggests that the Cavallis could not support him domestically and that he was sent from one place to another. All this must have been disquieting to the young man, and it is perhaps only natural that he should have sought refuge and consolation elsewhere, in some of the more decadent areas of seventeenth-century Venetian life. Almost certainly he began to gamble, and in the 1620's he contracted a number of debts.[15] Here at least it was the patrician Cavalli family who stood by him. Records imply that financial transactions such as loans and repayments were carried out at their house. At the end of his own life Cavalli made a generous bequest to the descendants of his patron, not only in acknowledgement of his gratitude for constant encouragement, but also, perhaps, in repayment for the ready help he had always received in an emergency ('et in particolare nelle mie urgenze').[16]

From these adolescent frolics there arose in 1630 a greater stability and maturity, probably for two reasons. The brutal plague brought by the Imperial troops who had sacked Mantua in 1638 swept through Venice with devastating results. Giustiniano Martinioni, revising Francesco Sansovino's *Venetia, città nobilissima, et singolare* in 1663, claimed that there had been 80,000 deaths in the Veneto. On 4 December 1630 the priests at SS. Giovanni e Paolo declared that their *maestro di grammatica* and all but one of their novices had died, and that Cavalli was not able to come to the church during the period of contagion.[17] They therefore relieved him of his duties. (Three months later, when the plague had receded, they did not reappoint Cavalli to his former post, but employed instead Carlo Fillago, the first organist at St. Mark's. This perhaps suggests that Cavalli's irresponsibility in the 1620's had also affected the discharge of his duties outside St. Mark's.) However, just as it was impossible to attend even places of worship, so the gambling houses too may have closed, at least temporarily, so reducing the temptations offered to the young Cavalli. But the second reason for Cavalli's greater maturity was matrimony. On 7 January 1630 he married Maria Sosomeno, a wealthy widow several years his senior. In so doing he acquired instant financial security, and also responsibility for Maria's large family of dependants, and furthermore the duty of administering her considerable territorial properties. At the end of her life Maria's will testified to the effectiveness with which he rose to these challenges. Through them he discovered and nurtured a flair for organisation, discipline and efficiency which remained with him for the rest of his life.

Maria Sosomeno was the daughter of Giulia da Canal and Domenico Loredani (the first of Giulia's three husbands), and after the death of her father she had been brought up under the guardianship of her uncle Claudio Sosomeno, the Bishop of Pola.[18] It was he who had supplied the generous dowry for her first marriage in 1617,[19] and when he died in 1622 he left all his possessions to her, having always loved her as a daughter ('da me amata come figlia').[20] Her first husband, Alvise Schiavina, was also well-connected, and during the 1620's received many handsome legacies.[21] These enabled him, in 1625, to buy a villa and estate at Gambarare, on the mainland towards Padua, for the large sum of 4000 ducats.[22] Maria Sosomeno and Alvise Schiavina had two children, Claudia and Pietro, before Schiavina died in June 1629.[23] Maria married Cavalli only six months later.

The marriage document between Cavalli and Maria Sosomeno does not survive, but the declaration of her dowry, dated 11 July 1630, states that the marriage had taken place seven months previously.[24] Maria's material contribution to the marriage was considerable. As well as various sums of 300 ducats, 250 ducats, 100 ducats and 1000 ducats (the last from her mother, promised to Maria at her first marriage, but apparently untouched because of Schiavina's own wealth), she possessed the whole property at Gambarare. Cavalli was to involve himself passionately with this prosperous estate. He extended it frequently, controlled its affairs and its profits, and for him it became a source of substantial income for the rest of his life. Maria Sosomeno was also to inherit property in Venice from her mother in 1644, and this too Cavalli administered for her, and enjoyed the profits that it yielded. Their marriage, though childless, was clearly successful and deeply affectionate. Cavalli not only looked after her and managed her affairs but also cared indirectly for the rest of her family. Her two children were apparently not part of their immediate household: Claudia was, as her mother had been on her own father's death, brought up by a close friend of the family, in this case Girolamo Mocenigo. (Mocenigo had been one of the executors of Claudio Sosomeno's will in 1624, together with Maria and her mother, and closely connected with their affairs ever since.[25] At Claudia's own subsequent marriage in 1643, it was Mocenigo who supplied the dowry.[26] It is even possible that the Mocenigo family was responsible for the original meeting betwen Cavalli and his wife, for it will be remembered that Cavalli had been lodging in the house of Alvise Mocenigo in 1620.) Maria's other child, Pietro, became a monk, Brother Giovanni Battista, at the Monastero di Santa Maria dei Carmini in 1637, and relinquished all his property and inheritances to his mother.[27] But Cavalli clearly felt concerned in all their activities, for among his papers at his own death some 40 years later were found his personal copies of documents (such as marriage contracts and wills) relating to Claudia and Pietro.

During the 1630's, Cavalli's musical activities and reputation continued to increase. In 1634 he was a contributor, with his 'Son ancora pargoletta', to a published collection of arias, where Monteverdi was again represented.[28] In 1635 his modest salary as a singer at St. Mark's was raised by 20 ducats to 100 per annum.[29] Two years later he was responsible for organising the music for the celebration of the Pentecost at the church of Spirito Santo.[30] In 1639, on the death of the second organist at St. Mark's, G. Pietro Berti, Cavalli competed for the post with three others. His rival competitors were Nicolo Fontei, Natal Monferrato and Giacomi Arigoni, but Cavalli apparently won the unanimous vote of Monteverdi and the auditioning Procurators and so secured the job with a salary of 140 ducats per year.[31] He joined Fillago, Rovetta *(Vice-maestro di cappella)* and Monteverdi, the impressive team of leaders under whom St. Mark's was enjoying a stable period of high musical standards. As if to celebrate his new appointment, in the following month Cavalli spent 28 ducats on a small piece of land adjacent to his Gambarare property.[32] This was the first of many such purchases of various sizes, which often coincided with a rise in salary or income as on this occasion.

Meanwhile, however, in the early months of 1637, one of the most important events in the history of music had taken place in Venice. An old comedy theatre, the Teatro San Cassiano, had been re-opened by a company of six singers and supporting instrumentalists, who had performed Francesco Manelli's opera, *Andromeda.*[33] Whereas this new art-form, of drama in continuous music, had hitherto been largely the property and privilege of the aristocratic few in the courts of Mantua, Florence and Rome, here it was presented to a wider cross-section of Venice's richly-varied population. *Andromeda* and its successor *La Maga Fulminata,* given by the same company in the following year, aroused in Venetian dramatists, composers and audiences alike a voracious appetite for opera, and were the source of an almost continuous flow of such works presented in Venetian theatres throughout the rest of the century.[34]

This arrival of opera was felicitously timed. Politically Venice was continuing to decline: for over a century repeated losses of territorial, maritime and trading power had emphasised the gradual disintegration of her world supremacy. Now the impending wars in Crete were to torture her for the next 30 years. Venice was ready for an all-embracing, all-engrossing diversion which would indulge her escapist longings; and opera provided it.

Cavalli was one of the first Venetian musicians to become involved in the new art-form. In 1638, only a year after the arrival of the Roman company, he was part of a group of theatrical enthusiasts who formed a company to present opera at the Teatro San Cassiano.[35] Among his immediate associates were the poet Orazio Persiani, the singer Felicita Uga, and the choreographer Giovanni Battista Balbi. The first outcome of the formation of this company was the opera *Le Nozze di Teti e di Peleo,* presented at San Cassiano on 20 January 1639. For Cavalli this was the beginning of a prolonged, prestigious and intensely arduous period of activity in Venetian opera houses. The effectiveness of his managerial capacity at San Cassiano is somewhat in doubt, with evidence suggesting that there were administrative difficulties during the theatre's early years,[36] but his connection with the establishment as a composer remained constant for another decade. After *Teti e Peleo* he wrote nine more operas for the house in ten years,[37] after which his association with it temporarily ceased during the theatre's six-year closure. Among these first San Cassiano works were two collaborations with the poet Francesco Busenello *(Gli amori d'Apollo e di Dafne* and *Didone)* in 1640 and 1641, and five consecutive operas with the young librettist Giovanni Faustini *(La Virtù de' strali d'Amore, Egisto, Ormindo, Titone* and *Doriclea)* in the years 1642 to 1645. He also collaborated with Faustini on *Euripo* in 1649 at the Teatro San Moisè, where he had earlier been involved in management,[38] and where his *Amore innamorato* (to a libretto by Fusconi) had been performed in 1642.[39] His last two operas for San Cassiano before his temporary departure from it were in collaboration with two new librettists. One was an outstanding success and the other an outstanding failure. His setting of Cicognini's *Giasone* (1649) was revived all over the country for the rest of the century;[40] but that of Minato's *Orimonte* (1650) was conspicuously unsuccessful, and ultimately rejected also by its librettist.[41] (Nicolo Minato was however later to become a close friend and collaborator of Cavalli, and their subsequent works were considerably more successful.) It is also conceivable that in this decade he worked on Monteverdi's last opera, *L'Incoronazione di Poppea* (with a Busenello libretto, given at the Teatro SS. Giovanni e Paolo in 1642), perhaps directed a revival of it in 1646 after the composer's death,[42] and supervised its transfer to other Italian cities including Naples in the early 1650's.

The advent of public opera, then, and the resulting flow of rapidly-opening theatres to accommodate it, and of rapidly-emerging dramatists, composers, singers and choreographers to perform it, considerably shifted Cavalli's own musical emphasis from the church to the theatre. During the 1640's he, his librettists and his audiences all discovered his profound theatrical sense; and the brisk succession of those first 12 works in 11 years testifies to the ability with which he was able to keep abreast of the demand for his operas. But, as was paradoxically the case throughout his career, opera was for Cavalli almost a luxurious professional extra. It clearly occupied much of his time and energies, but the material profits that he gained from it were unreliable and probably as yet insubstantial, and it must be remembered that his chief source of income came, as always, from his appointment at St. Mark's and from his administration of his wife's property at Gambarare. Certainly his non-operatic activities in these same years continued to increase his reputation and his standard of living. On three occasions his salary as an organist was raised: by 20 ducats on 11 January 1643, 20 more on 19 February 1645, and ten more on 14 July 1647, making a total of 190 ducats per year.[43] In 1645 he contributed his 'O quam suavis' to another miscellaneous collection of sacred motets in Venice.[44] In the same year Giovanni Battista Volpe published a collection of madrigals by his uncle Giovanni Rovetta (who had succeeded Monteverdi as *maestro di cappella* at St. Mark's) and dedicated it to Cavalli.[45] Both Volpe and his uncle were naturally close associates of Cavalli. Volpe was later to deputise for him at the organ of St. Mark's when Cavalli was called to France, and later still joined him as the second organist on the departure of Massimilio Neri in 1665. (And, like Cavalli, he too eventually became *maestro di cappella* towards the end of his life.) Volpe's dedication of the madrigal volume was eloquent in its praise, for it declared that Cavalli's performing talents at the organ of St. Mark's were matched by his composing talents in sacred, secular and dramatic music ('e nelle Chiese, e nelle Camere, e ne' Teatri'). He went on to extol three further qualities: Cavalli's ability to set his texts to noble music, to sing them incomparably and to accompany them with delicate precision. So Cavalli's proficiency in all musical fields had been publicly acknowledged.[46]

In 1646 Cavalli temporarily intervened as organist at the church of S. Caterina.[47] Two years later, in January 1648, he and his wife rented a large house in the parish of S. Tomà, at a rent of 27 ducats per quarter.[48] They were to live there for the rest of their lives. This move to a fashionable part of the city, at a rental well over half his organist's salary, certainly suggests that Cavalli's non-ecclesiastical activities were becoming more profitable. But from the point of view of his personal life, the 1640's were sad years for Cavalli. His father Giovanni Battista Caletti died in Crema in 1642. There had been little if any family communication between Crema and Venice, and Cavalli did not even learn of his father's death for several months. On travelling to Crema, he discovered that his father had left debts which exceeded the value of his legacies. He therefore chose to renounce the bequest made to him, and to consign its disentanglements to his sister Diambra Caterina and her husband Faustineo Medici.[49] It cannot be denied that this incident was one of the least attractive in the whole of his life. Such ungenerous behaviour could perhaps be partially explained by his perpetual separation from his family since the age of 14. Absence may in this case have led to antagonism, manifesting itself in an unsympathetic gesture.

In 1643, on 29 November, Monteverdi died. Cavalli was doubtless involved in the large double funeral service held for him first in St. Mark's and later in the church of the Frari, where he was buried,[50] and must have felt profound grief at the loss of so great a teacher and friend. Later he was able to acknowledge more publicly his gratitude to his late colleague. He edited Monteverdi's *Messa a 4 voci, et salmi* in 1650, and was responsible for the revivals of *Poppea* in the early years of the decade. On 20 October 1644 his mother-in-law Guilia Canal also died.[51] In her will she left to her daughter a house in the Corte Contarina, which Cavalli administered for her, as he did all her other properties.[52] Two further deaths followed in the next two years: those of Maria's daughter Claudia (who had married Bortolo Barbieri only in 1644), and of Claudia's own daughter Bianca. It is conceivable that Maria herself was also ill. She made a will on 5 July 1647, which, though not her last, left everything to her husband.[53] At the end of 1651, Cavalli's operatic colleague of ten years' standing, Giovanni Faustini, died,[54] and finally Maria herself died on 16 September 1652.[55] Her last will, made on 11 March 1651, is a comparatively long document, but her legacies were simple and straightforward. [56] She left 20 ducats each to Giulio Alberghini, her half-brother (by her mother's second marriage), and to Catterina Abbati, her half-sister (by her mother's third marriage); and 100 ducats to 'Andriana figliola del Sig. Lorenzo Zordan . . . dalle Gambarare', in case she should neither marry nor enter a nunnery. (Andriana was presumably a young girl in her service at Gambarare, and if she were to marry or enter a nunnery, then the legacy would be reduced to five ducats.[57]) The rest of her possessions she left to her 'carissimo consorte', in loving gratitude for all he had been and done for her and her family; for during the time of their marriage he had supported and assisted all her own relations, including her mother, brother, sister, aunt and children, according to the occasion and the need. For this reason, she declared, she left him 'assoluto patrone' of all that she possessed, and did so with all her heart.[58]

Cavalli did not re-marry after Maria's death. He continued the assistance Maria had promised to Bortolo Barbieri, widower of his step-daughter Claudia,[59] he continued occasionally to help her other relatives when in need,[60] and he continued to administer all the possessions that he now owned. But, perhaps curiously, Cavalli's professional career was unaffected by the quick succession of deaths of people close to him. Some 40 years earlier, Monteverdi's life had temporarily crumbled with the death of his own wife, but Cavalli undeniably continued to approach the peak of his career. His enormous activity in all musical spheres was being repaid by widespread performances of his works and continuous far-reaching renown. In the 1650's he wrote 14 more operas, published his largest collection of sacred music, spent a considerable sum of money on extending his property at Gambarare, and, at the end of the decade, received what was doubtless the greatest honour of his life, an invitation from Cardinal Mazarin to compose the opera for the marriage between Louis XIV and Maria Theresa of Spain.

Back in May, 1650, Giovanni Faustini, with whom Cavalli had produced five operas in the previous decade, found himself in financial difficulties. In an attempt to improve the situation he hired the smallest theatre in Venice, the Teatro Sant' Apollinare, from a family of merchants named Ceroni.[61] In a business partnership with the noblemen Alvise Duodo and Marc'Antonio Corraro, Faustini intended to perform two of his operas there each season, and so renewed his collaboration with Cavalli who was at the time energetically involved with establishing an operatic transfer system between Venice and Naples. The theatre opened in 1651 with their *Oristeo* and *Rosinda,* and for the following season they planned *Calisto* and *Eritrea.* But Faustini's death on 19 December 1651, immediately before the new season was to start, naturally terminated the Cavalli-Faustini monopoly of the theatre, although *Calisto* and *Eritrea* duly opened. Faustini was succeeded in the administration of Sant' Apollinare by his brother Marco, a lawyer. He continued the collaboration with Duodo and Corraro, and these three men became a powerful triumvirate of theatrical impresarios, moving into ever larger opera houses with increasing success.[62] But because of the considerable financial disorder in which Giovanni Faustini had left Sant' Apollinare, Marco Faustini was unable to secure Cavalli's services there for three seasons. (Indeed, he was compelled to present two straight dramas, with music only in prologues and interludes, in the 1653 season, before he could again afford a musical company.)

In 1653 Cavalli set Melosio's *Orione* (a libretto he had originally turned down when he and Melosio were working together at S. Moisè[63]) for the young Hapsburg Ferdinando IV in Milan. In the same year he also began his connection with one of the largest Venetian opera houses, the Teatro SS. Giovanni e Paolo. *Veremonda* of 1653, to a libretto by Giulio Strozzi,[64] was followed in 1654 by *Ciro*. Both works were imported from Naples where they had had their first performances: for *Ciro* Cavalli wrote only the prologue and various musical additions.[65] For the same theatre he collaborated with Minato on *Xerse* in 1655, with Busenello (his colleague of thirteen years previously) on *Statira* in 1656, and with Minato again on *Artemisia* in 1657. Meanwhile he had set Moniglia's libretto *Ipermestra* for Florence in 1654 (although it was not performed until 1658[66]), and Marco Faustini had been pressing him to return to Sant' Apollinare. Cavalli eventually agreed to do so; but in a letter to Marco Faustini of 23 July 1654 he complained of his dealings with Alvise Duodo on a past occasion, clearly showing reluctance to continue working with Faustini if Duodo persisted in his unsatisfactory practices.[67] The letter is one of the most telling examples of Cavalli's strong business acumen: he is firm in his ideas and desires, and articulate in expressing them. Somehow Marco Faustini succeeded in appeasing Cavalli and in engaging his services for the following season. The result was *Erismena,* Cavalli's setting of a libretto by the young lawyer and writer Aurelio Aureli. This production opened on Boxing Day 1655, and so began the 1656 season.

Thereafter Marco Faustini became a crucial factor in Cavalli's Venetian opera career. By 1657, together with Duodo and Corraro, he had become totally disenchanted with Sant' Apollinare, partly because of its severe physical limitations, and partly because of prolonged litigation concerning its finances. So when the Tron family, who owned the Teatro San Cassiano, offered Marco Faustini and his associates the running of their theatre at its re-opening, they were happy to accept.[68] Their first move was to engage Cavalli as musical director, and on 24 July 1658 they contracted him to San Cassiano for a period of three years.[69] The four clauses of the contract state, first, that Cavalli should provide one opera a year for the three years, making all scores, copies and parts at his own expense; secondly, that he should be at all rehearsals to make the necessary additions, deletions and alterations; thirdly, that during this period of three years Cavalli might not write for any other Venetian theatre, although he might accept engagements outside Venice; and finally that he should direct all performances from the first harpsichord (for no extra pay) and provide a deputy at his own expense should he be indisposed through illness. In payment for all this, Cavalli would receive 400 ducats a year—exactly twice as much as he was being paid as an organist at St Mark's. This considerable fee, for only one opera a year, is a clear measure of Cavalli's reputed value in 1658. In complete contrast to the rate at which he had been composing even at the beginning of the same decade, he was now in the commanding position of being able to produce operas at a comparatively leisurely pace. For the 1659 season he wrote *Antioco* with Minato, and followed it in the next year with *Elena*, a completion by the same librettist of an unfinished text by his late colleague Giovanni Faustini.

It was at this point that Cavalli received his invitation to Paris from the French court, as a result of which he deferred the completion of his contract with Marco Faustini and did not provide the third opera until 1664. But before considering this large event in Cavalli's life, which was probably the turning-point in his whole operatic career, it is necessary first to complete the tally of achievements in the 1650's with a summary of his non-operatic activities. For these, no less than his operas, indicate the solid fame and affluence that Cavalli was currently enjoying, and contribute to the undeniable fact that he was now at the very peak of his career.

When, in 1650, Cavalli had edited Monteverdi's posthumously-published *Messa a 4 voci, et salmi,* he had included his own six-part setting of the *Magnificat*. On 14 January 1653 his salary as an organist had been raised by ten ducats to 200 per annum.[70] (It was his fourth pay-rise in ten years.) Two years later, on 10 October 1655 he spent twelve ducats on land at Gambarare, purchasing it from his immediate neighbours there, the Roseto family.[71] Five months after that, he spent no less than 1500 ducats on considerably more land for his Gambarare estate, this time buying from Francesco Rota.[72] (This important transaction was interestingly handled for him by Minato, who, like Marco Faustini and Aurelio Aureli, was a practising lawyer.[73]) In the same year he published a large collection of sacred music, his *Musiche Sacre.*[74] He dedicated it to Cardinal Giovanni Carlo de' Medici, the President of the Accademici Immobili in Florence, for whom he had written *Ipermestra* two years previously. (Cavalli stated in the dedication that he had already written works for the Cardinal; he referred to 'altre Compositioni . . . già reso avezzo l'udito alle mie debolezze'.) In the preface to the volume,[75] Cavalli confessed that it was rare for him to commit his compositions to print, but that on this occasion he had been persuaded to do so by Alessandro Vincenti, the publisher. After various humilities and courtesies, Cavalli went on to give some typically punctilious directions to the reader as to how the 16 pieces in the volume should be performed, and these were supplemented by a similar note in the part books from the printer to the performers. Here again is evidence of Cavalli's clarity of mind. In the same year Cavalli also contributed three more motets to a collection published by B. Marcesso, *La Sacra Corona.* (Two of these were later reprinted in a collection by M. Silvani, Bologna, in 1668.) Finally, it was in this year that Cavalli began to keep personal and meticulous accounts,[76] presumably in addition to those being kept by his financial agents. He continued these right up until his death, the only gaps in them being for the financial years 1661 to 1663, when he was absent in France.

The extent of Cavalli's realised talents at the end of the 1650's, then, was enormous, and his comfortable reputation at home was equally matched by an ever-spreading renown outside Venice.[77] So it was perhaps not at all surprising that the cosmopolitan French statesman Cardinal Mazarin singled him out from all other major European composers and invited him to participate in the celebrations of his sovereign's marriage.[78] On 9 June 1659 Mazarin and his colleague Pimantel had signed the Treaty of Paris, which led to the Peace of the Pyrenees three months later. In order to seal this diplomatic agreement, Mazarin arranged the marriage between King Louis XIV and the Infanta of Spain, and planned to celebrate their wedding in the most extravagant possible style. He ordered the building of a new theatre in the Tuileries to accommodate the operatic festivities, and, advised by the castrato Atto Melani, who was employed at the French court and was a close friend and associate of Mazarin, he summoned the Modenese architect and designer Gaspare Vigarani to come and build it, with his two sons Carlo and Lodovico. He then asked his colleague, the abbot Francesco Buti, to write a libretto for a new opera to be performed in this splendid house, and also to write to Cavalli in Venice to seek his collaboration. (Here again Mazarin was probably influenced by Melani, who had sung in a Florentine performance of Cavalli's *Xerse* in 1655.) Buti initially wavered; it seems that he was unenthusiastic about collaborating with a well-respected Italian composer, and tried to persuade Mazarin to invite instead the relatively unknown harpist, Giovanni Carlo Rossi (brother of the composer Luigi Rossi, whose *Orfeo* had been performed in Paris in 1647). But Mazarin persisted in his determination to secure Cavalli's attendance, and in due course Cavalli was invited. Despite the great honour that Cavalli must have felt at such a invitation, he initially refused it. In a letter to Buti, written on 22 August 1659, he thanked the abbot most graciously for his generous invitation, but stated that he felt unable to accept it for reasons of age, health and arduous occupation (both professional and personal) in Venice.[79] It seems that there were also financial considerations: Cavalli's letter politely refers to an original promise of 'mille doble', which has now been reduced. Buti forwarded Cavalli's letter to Mazarin, who in his reply expressed disappointment and suggested that Buti should contact 'celuy mesme d'Inspruck'; this was almost certainly Cavalli's closest operatic rival, Antonio Cesti. At this point the narrative becomes obscure, for not all the documentation of the international transaction survives. But by the following November,

Buti had written back to Cavalli offering him even larger sums of money than those originally quoted, and Cavalli had agreed to go. Whether it was the increased fee that made Cavalli change his mind, or whether it was the knowledge that if he did not go, then his rival Cesti would almost certainly receive the many honours, will probably never be known. But Mazarin was clearly delighted, and in a letter to Buti of 16 November declared that he felt 'bien aise' to learn of Cavalli's acceptance.[80]

Before Cavalli could make his final arrangements for departure, he had to be temporarily released from his duties at St. Mark's. The official French request was made to the Procurators by the French ambassador in Venic, the Archbishop d'Embrun, on 9 March. (By this time Cavalli had already worked for him: on 25 January 1660 d'Embrun had celebrated the Peace of the Pyrenees in the church of SS. Giovanni e Paolo with a Mass and Te Deum written by Cavalli.) Following the ambassador's written request,[81] the Procurators in due course decided to release Cavalli for this important occasion. On 11 April 1661 they declared that he had been given leave to go to France and that his post at St. Markk's would be held for him until his return. They went on to stipulate that during Cavalli's absence Giovanni Battista Volpe should deputise for him.[82] Later still, on 26 April, in response to a further request from the French ambassador, they also released two singers, the castrato Giovanni Caliari and the tenor Giovanni Agostino Poncelli, from their duties at St. Mark's.[83] These two men travelled with Cavalli, as did another young man, Giacomo da Murano. He was probably taken as a copyist, for, although it is certain that he travelled to France with Cavalli,[84] there is no indication in the cast lists of the two operas subsequently staged there that he had performed as a singer. For the period of his absence, Cavalli left the administration of his affairs to the hands of his friend, the notary Claudio Paulini.[85]

Travelling via Innsbruck and possibly also Munich,[86] Cavalli arrived in Paris in July 1660. (By this time the marriage itself had already taken place, at St Jean-de-Luz on 9 June.) Immediately he was confronted by the first of the many problems that were to beset his stay in Paris. The new theatre at the Tuileries was not going to be completed on schedule, and for the proposed celebratory Carnival season a different building had to be found and some other work (not the new opera) performed. For this, an old opera of Cavalli's was revived. *Xerse* was chosen (presumably again at Atto Melani's instigation) and Cavalli's first tasks were to restructure it and adapt it to Parisian tastes. The standard three acts of the Venetian format were therefore redistributed into five; ballets were organised to be performed between them; and the prominent castrato part of the original title role was given to a baritone, while Atto Melani repeated his performance of the other male protagonist, Arsamene. The opera was performed in the gallery of the Louvre on 22 November. But despite Cavalli's supreme efforts at adapting it to its new environment, it gave considerably less pleasure than did the intermediary ballets. These were composed by none other than Lully, who, while rapidly making sure that he was becoming a great favourite at court, was present throughout the period of Cavalli's stay, and quite possibly sabotaged Cavalli's reputation among the musicians with whom he was working.

This unfortunate situation was repeated when *Ercole Amante* (Cavalli's setting of Buti's text) was finally performed in the new theatre at the Tuileries on 7 February 1662. (In the meantime, Cavalli's chief supporter, Cardinal Mazarin, had died on 9 March 1661.) Again Cavalli exerted enormous energies in adapting his style to an essentially alien set of conventions. The quasi-classical subject (which must by now have seemed quite anachronistic to Cavalli) was again dispersed in five acts; there were large choruses and crowd scenes (which likewise were by this time completely contrary to Venetian operatic taste); and Cavalli scored it heavily. The basic problems of a different musical and dramatic convention were further exacerbated by the Vigaranis' theatre. The huge auditorium was spectacular and impressive, and seated 7000 people comfortably; but the acoustic was disastrous, and French audiences were still unaccustomed to remaining silent throughout opera performances, with the result that most of the spectators were unable to hear Cavalli's music. The Venetian ambassador in Paris, Luigi Grimani, reported this disappointing fact back to the Senate, the only consolation being that the work had offered some enjoyment during rehearsals.[87]

The outcome, then, was that Cavalli's music failed to please. Lully's ballets, on the other hand, were danced by the King and Queen themselves, among others, and naturally received all the praise and attention. Cavalli's disappointment was understandably bitter. The usual court presentations and superficial honours had duly been bestowed upon him, but he had encountered an antagonism of a type which he had never met elsewhere. Clearly, he had been on unsure territory from the start. Indeed, as a foreigner presenting a foreign opera, sung by foreign singers to an essentially dilettante but obstinately patriotic audience, he had experienced similar artistic problems to those of Handel in London a century later. But whereas Handel at least had the initial support of fanatical audiences who supported his productions through the early years until Italian opera had become a regular feature of London entertainment, Cavalli had had only one opportunity to succeed, and the combination of acoustical problems with personal jealousies meant that he had failed to do so.

By August 1662 Cavalli was back in Venice, much distraught from his experience. The prolonged struggles and the gradual disintegration of his morale had produced in him the effect that the deaths of his family and friends ten years earlier had not. Thereafter he viewed operatic offers, even those from his oldest associates, with reserve. Marco Faustini, who was now managing the Teatro SS. Giovanni e Paolo with Duodo and Corraro, was clearly hoping to secure the services of both Cavalli and Minato there for the 1663 season. As far as he was concerned Cavalli's operas were still in demand, and during the composer's absence his *Eritrea* had been revived in the Teatro S. Salvatore in 1661. But, in spite of all Cavalli's loyalties to Marco Faustini and a genuine desire to work for him again, he turned down Faustini's offer. In a letter of 8 August he stated that he never again wished to write theatrical works: 'Sono ritornato di Francia con fermissimo proponimento di non affaticarmi più in opere teatrali'.[88] He went on to make the half-hearted suggestion that *Ercole Amante* should be seen in Venice, a suggestion which Faustini nevertheless turned down. Later he also claimed that the pressures of his business affairs (presumably those relating to Gambarare) gave him little time to write operas.[89] But in due course he was persuaded to collaborate again with Minato, and for the 1664 season they produced *Scipione Affricano* at SS. Giovanni e Paolo, following this in the next two years with *Muzio Scevola* and *Pompeo Magno* at S. Salvatore. In 1666 *Giasone* wa revived at San Cassiano, and on 29 June 1667 Marco Faustini contracted Cavalli to write a new opera at SS. Giovanni e Paolo, for a fee of 400 ducats.[90] The proposed work was a revision by Aureli of a libretto entitled *Eliogabalo.* Cavalli duly set the text, but it was never performed. Instead the 1668 Carnival season presented Aureli's new text of *Eliogabalo* (completely different from its predecessor) set by the young composer Boretti. The reasons for this last-minute substitution are not clear, but Marco Faustini also left SS. Giovanni e Paolo just before the Carnival season opened, and Cavalli's loyalties to this old friend and colleague may have caused him to remove his opera. It is however more likely that Cavalli's operatic style was simply no longer abreast of current trends. His particular talent, the ability to enhance a dramatic text by dramatic music and so to produce a fluent and closely integrated combination of music and drama, was no longer relevant. By now audiences wanted 'exhibition' arias sung by their favourite soloists. Recitative, and therefore dramatic action, were considered to be a mere link between these showcases of technical virtuosity, and Cavalli's style was unable to adapt itself to such an essentially non-dramatic aesthetic. The unfortunate *Eliogabalo* incident was, even more unhappily, repeated in 1673, when Cavalli was asked to set Bussani's libretto *Massenzio* for the Teatro S. Salvatore. The opera was actually in rehearsal before it was decided that the arias *per se* did not achieve the desired standard. It too was scrapped, and the younger man Antonio Sartorio rapidly provided a substitute score to the same text.[91] So Cavalli's last performed opera was written, not for Venice, but for Piacenza. In 1669 he collaborated with Ivanovich on *Coriolano,* performed to celebrate the birth of Edoardo II. But clearly Cavalli's operas were out of fashion; and while they may still have been a draw for aristocratic Italian audiences (*Coriolano* was performed before the Duke of Mantua), the devastating directness of the Venetian public audiences ceased to demand them. It was probably in these last operatic years that Cavalli employed a scribe to make neat copies of all his scores, as if he himself was aware that his involvement with theatrical affairs had drawn to a close.[92]

During the 1660's Cavalli's advancing age became more apparent, and there were signs of failing health. In his letter to Buti of 1659 he had vividly described his inability to work for more than so many hours without becoming ill.[93] He certainly grew more forgetful, and neglected to pay people who had acted for him professionally.[94] But there was also a mellowing, for in these latter years he showed more compassion to his family in Crema. At last he renewed contact with his sisters; he had visited them on his return from France, and now he welcomed them to Venice, adopted their servant Maddalena, and ultimately organised their burial in his own parish church of S. Lorenzo.

Outside the opera house Cavalli's activities continued to flourish, and he turned fuller attentions to his duties at St. Mark's and to the administration of his property. On the death of Rovetta in 1668 he finally became *maestro di cappella* on 20 November.[95] With characteristic practicality, one of his first moves was to complain officially to the Procurators about the inconvenience caused to his musicians in reaching the north loft. As a result of his complaint an extra stairway was erected leading to the loft from the Sacristy.[96] It seems that he also composed a great deal of music for the Basilica. There is evidence (though no surviving material) of a Mass, a Magnificat and some motets in 1671, and, four years later, three further Masses (two in four parts and one in five), two hymns, two motets and a Requiem, of which only the Requiem survives.[97] These considerable energies directed into his new post were matched by similar activity as a property-owner. On 9 September 1665 he spent six ducats on a small piece of land from the neighbouring Roseto family at Gambarare, and in the following January made an enormous increase in his estate, spending 1200 ducats on land bought from Marc' Antonio Pontin. Three more acquisitions followed these: on 16 February 1671, on 30 May 1673, and on 9 September 1675.[98]

On 8 March 1673 Cavalli remade his will (stating that he had already made it twice, before and after his visit to France).[99] In it he outlined elaborate arrangements for Requiem masses to be sung for the repose of his own soul. These arrangements were repeated in his final will, dated 12 March 1675.[100] His last published work consisted of three sets of Vespers in eight parts, which he dedicated to the current Doge, Nicolo Sagredo. On 14 January 1676 he died in his home in San Tomà. According to the directions in his will, he was buried in the church of S. Lorenzo, beside his wife and his two sisters, at the altar erected for his wife's uncle, Bishop Claudio Sosomeno. He was succeeded as *maestro di cappella* by Natal Monferrato, who had been *vice-maestro* since 1647,[102] and who was elected by the Procurators with an extremely narrow majority over Legrenzi and P. A. Ziani.[103]

Cavalli's highly detailed will was published on the day of his death by the Notary Claudio Paulini, who had acted for Cavalli and his family for several years.[104] Much of it repeated the provisions he had made in his penultimate will for the Masses to be said after his death. On the eighth day after his death, a Requiem Mass was to be sung in S. Lorenzo by the choir and musicians of St. Mark's. Cavalli stipulated that this Requiem should be specially composed by his successor, or, if the successor had not yet been appointed, by the current *vice-maestro.* (In either case, this would have been Monferrato.) 75 ducats from his estate were to cover the cost of this occasion. The 12-part instrumental band was to be made up of two violins, four violas, two cornetts, two theorboes, trombones, bassoon, violone and three organs. Besides this, 60 more ducats were to pay for another Requiem Mass to be sung twice a year, once in St. Mark's and once in S. Lorenzo. This was an eight-part Requiem of his own composition, requiring also a violone (to be played by a Signor Paolo Masina, the only player to be named in the list of instruments for the first Requiem). For both these Masses, Cavalli left the clearest possible instructions as to how the sum of money allotted to the occasions should be divided among the participants. Having no family or relatives of his own, Cavalli then bequeathed the majority of his possessions and real estate to the Monastery of S. Lorenzo. The investments from the sale of his property should be in the name of 'Comissaria di Francesco Cavalli'. He appointed as his executors three of his friends: Giovanni Caliari (or Calegari, the singer who had accompanied him to France and who was a close friend), Antonio Fustinoni and Angelo dall'Olio. For four years these three men should share the profits yielded by two of his estates, that is, the main property at Gambarare and the large addition he made to it in 1656. (Cavalli added that his servant, Francesco Covella, should also partake of these profits, since he would still be responsible for the running of the house.) After four years, these estates were then to be transferred to the patrician Cavalli family, in recognition of the great favours and generosity he had always received from them. If the male line of the Cavalli family should not be continued, then the property was to be returned to S. Lorenzo as originally directed. Both the Cavalli family and his executors should, while they occupied the property, continue his custom of distributing flour and wine to the poor on All Souls' Day, and also to his servant Maddalena from Crema. The large additions he had made to his property in 1666 (the purchase of land from Pontin) was to go to

Paulini himself for as long as he lived, as an indication of gratitude and friendship, and after his death it should revert to S. Lorenzo, as should all the other Gambarare properties.

At his death Cavalli also possessed property in Crema. The first of these, his own family's house,[105] was left to G. B. Lunetto, the son of his cousin. When the male line of his family died out, the property was then to be transferred to the hospital of the Pietà in Crema. The second property, some land near the Porte d'Ombriano, was left to Signor Paolo Medici, the husband of his late sister Diambra Caterina;[106] and it was to continue through the male line of his family, or else be transferred to the Hospital di Dio in Crema.

After these large distributions of property and estate, Cavalli's will then made several smaller bequests. His pupil, friend and executor Caliari was to receive all his manuscript music: church music, operas, and smaller works. Certain other benefactions are notable. He left 100 ducats to each of the four hospitals in Venice (these were the Pietà, the Incurabili, the Derelitti and the Mendicanti, and all were establishments for teaching singing to girls). His servant Maddalena of Crema received 800 ducats, against her marrying or entering a nunnery, together with all the furniture from his house in San Tomà. Two of his pupils, the nuns Francesca Grimani and Betta Mocenigo, received a spinet and some pictures, and another spinet was bequeathed to the organ-builder, Francesco Megrini. All his servants, including his boatman and barber, were remembered, and his friends received small objects such as silver saucers and other articles from the house. Clearly, Cavalli distributed his estate with the same clear-minded care that he had exercised in accumulating it.

As decreed in the will, Claudio Paulini occupied the large area of land that Cavalli had acquired in 1666, until his death on 24 February 1684. It then passed to S. Lorenzo on 10 April.[107] Similarly, his three executors enjoyed the use of the main Gambarare property for four years, renting out the land and sharing the profits.[108] Thereafter it passed to Giovanni (Zuanne) Cavalli, the son of Cavalli's original patron, and from him to his son Federico (Ferigo). It stayed with the Cavalli family until the death of this Federico on 2 March 1730,[109] when, since he had no male heirs, it passed back to the Monastery of S. Lorenzo on 17 April.[110]

Immediately after Cavalli's death, an inventory was made of the contents of his house in San Tomà and of his papers.[111] Among the interesting articles appearing in this scrupulously detailed list are the three spinets, portraits of Cavalli himself, his wife and the Bishop Sosomeno (lamentably none of these has survived), several other pictures, various silver articles embossed with the arms of the Cavalli family, and three collections of music. The itemised list of Cavalli's 'scritture' includes the tantalising mention of two letters from the 'Abbate Butij', dated 23 and 24 April, but no year is given.

These two lists of Cavalli's possessions and of his papers at the time of his death confirm the impressions of the man's character inferred from the rest of the evidence. He clearly had a strong business flair for organisation and administration. He had come into large amounts of property almost by accident at a comparatively young age, but he had developed and expanded these over the years according to the state of his own income, both earned and unearned. His long life had been arduous, rewarding, and possibly somewhat lonely. Though he was doubtless surrounded by a loyal circle of friends, it is conspicuous that his successes were achieved entirely as a result of his own personal efforts. Even commercially he was something of a lone wolf. His strong administrative capacity was fruitful only when he operated alone: any business undertaking that he entered as part of a syndicate, for example the managing of the Teatro San Cassiano in its early operatic years, was distinctly unsuccessful. It is undeniable that he had a certain amount of luck, principally in his encounter with Federico Cavalli in Crema and then in his marriage to an extremely wealthy woman; but his own considerable talents enabled him to make the best use of his good fortune. Indeed, it is tempting to draw a parallel between his approach to the composition and performance of an opera, and his approach to life. When a dramatist provided him with a good text, he enhanced it with good dramatic music to make an aggregate which exceeded the sum of its parts. Similarly, in his life, he was able to apply his gifts and capabilities to the fullest exploitation of almost every situation, with the result that his life, too, was something of a success story. And his contribution to the history of music was lasting and profound.

NOTES

1. For details of the Caletti family history, and later for an assessment of Cavalli's operatic career, see: T. Wiel: 'Francesco Cavalli e la musica scenica' in *Nuovo Archivio Veneto* XXVIII (Venice, 1914), pp.106–150.
2. Lodovico Canobio: *Annali in proseguimento alla storia di Alemanio Fino* ed. G. Solera (Milan, 1849).
3. Diambra Caterina was the seventh-born child, and the third to be thus named (after her two grandmothers).
4. Crema, Archivio parocchiale di S. Benedetto; Atti di nascità, Vol.VI.
5. 'Fioriva . . . Giovanni Battista Caletto nostro Cremasco, che hà ben per lo spazio di quaranta e più anni governata con titolo di maestro di Capella la pubblica musica del Duomo'. Wiel, in 'Francesco Cavalli . . .', *op. cit.*, disbelieves Canobio's statement that G.B. Caletti was actually *maestro di cappella* for so many years. The title page of his madrigal publication in 1604, however, describes him in this capacity (see note 6, below), and it is known that he died in 1642 (see note 49, below).
6. *Madrigali a cinque voci di Gio: Battista Calletti detto il Bruno, Maestro di capella nel Domo di Crema. Libro Primo.* (Venice, Amadino, 1604).
7. The dedication, dated 16 May 1604, states that G.B. Caletti had taught her singing and the lute.
8. *Il primo libro de madrigali a cinque voci di Gio: Battista Leonetti, Organista in Santo Agostino di Crema* (Venice, Vincenti, 1607).
9. ASV, Procuratori di S. Marco, Procuratia de supra, fasc.35: Decreti & terminazioni, reg.141, f.53v. See Appendix III/i for the text of the Procurators' declaration.
10. ASV, Cancelleria Inferiore, 1615–1623, f.74.
11. ASV, SS. Giovanni e Paolo, reg.XII (1617–1636), f.60. See: D. Arnold: 'Francesco Cavalli: some recently discovered documents' in *ML* XLVI (1965), pp.50–55.
12. *Ghirlanda Sacra scielta da diversi eccelentissimi Compositori de varii Motetti a voce sola* (Venice, Gardano, 1625).
13. ASV, Scuola di S Rocco, f.168, cauzioni (1627–8).
14. The declaration of Cavalli's appointment as organist to SS. Giovanni e Paolo states: '. . . Pietro Francheschini Calletto Bruni da Crema qual habita in case dell' Ill.mo Sig.r Alvise Mocenigo . . .' ASV, SS. Giovanni e Paolo, reg.XII (1617–1636), f.60.
15. ASV, S. Lorenzo,b.24, BB, cc.1–16: statements of Cavalli debts to a Signor Gio: Maria Rimondi.
16. See complete text of will in Wiel 'Francesco Cavalli . . .', *op. cit.*
17. ASV, SS. Giovanni e Paolo, reg.XII (1617–1636), f.206. See Arnold, *op. cit.*
18. Giulia da Canal's father, Domenico Canal, was 'consanguineo'

(blood-relative) of Claudio Sosomeno. See ASV, S. Lorenzo, b.24, B, f.54.
19. ASV, S. Lorenzo, b.23, 21, ff.26–28v. (Marriage contract and declaration of dowry, dated 11 August 1617).
20. ASV, S. Lorenzo, b.24, DD, ref. 24 March 1622 (Sosomeno's will). He died two days later.
21. Listed in ASV, S. Lorenzo, b.24, AA.
22. Declaration of purchase: ASV, S. Lorenzo, b.24, AA, ff.60–66, dated 3 July 1625.
23. The exact date of his death is unclear, but ASV, S. Lorenzo, b.24, DD, ref.XX24 (11 September 1629) suggests that it had been in the previous June.
24. ASV, Notarile Claudio Paulini, Atti, b.3403, f.466–468v. Summarised also in: ASV, S. Lorenzo, b.24, DD, ref. XX25.
25. He is mentioned in the marriage contract between Cavalli and Maria Sosomeno (*ibid.*) as an administrator of Maria's affairs.
26. ASV, S. Lorenzo, b.23, 21, ff.30–30v.
27. ASV, S. Lorenzo, b.24, DD, ref.XX26 (18 August 1637).
28. *Arie di Diversi raccolte da A. Vincenti* (Venice, 1634).
29. ASV, Procuratori di S. Marco, Procuratia de supra, fasc.35: Decreti e terminazioni, reg.143, f.105v.
30. ASV, Fondo Monastero Spirito Santo.
31. ASV, Procuratori di S. Marco, Procuratia Chiesa, b.91: proc.207, f.41. Natal Monferrato was in fact to be appointed *vice-maestro di capella* in 1647. See: F. Caffi: *Storia della Musica Sacra nella già Capella Duc le di San Marco à Venezia 1318–1797* (Venice, 1854), pp.55–6.
32. ASV, S. Lorenzo, b.24, BB, f.4.
33. The Teatro San Cassiano had been closed since 1629 when it had been damaged by fire. See:
L.N. Galvani: *I teatri musicali di Venezia nel secolo XVII* (Milan, 1878), p.17.
34. For a complete list of operas performed in Venice in the seventeenth century, see: G.C. Bonlini: *Le glorie della poesia e della musica contenute nell' esatta notizia de' Teatri della città di Venezia* (Venice, 1730).
35. ASV, Monastero di S. Maria dell'Orazion a Malamocco, b.3. See: G. Morelli and T. Walker: 'Tre controversie intorno al S. Cassiano' in *Venezia e il melodrama nel seicento* (Florence, 1976), pp.97–120.
36. *ibid.*
37. See complete list of operas, Appendix I.
38. See: N. Pirrotta: 'Il caval zoppo e il vetturino. Cronache di Parnasso, 1642' in *Collectanea historia musicae* IV (1960), pp.215–226.
39. Fusconi, secretary of the Accademia degli Incogniti, had reworked the libretto from an original by his colleague Pietro Michiele, who in turn had taken the subject from Gio: Francesco Loredano. See:
L. Bianconi and T. Walker: 'Dalla *Finta Pazza* alla *Veremonda:* Storie di

Febiharmonici' in *RIM* X (1975), p.421, note 175.

40. See complete list of revivals in Appendix I.

41. From his *Antioco* (1659) onwards, Minato tended to list his previous works in the prefaces to new librettos; but he always began with *Xerse* (1655), his second opera.

42. For the arguments for and against this 1646 revival of *Poppea*, see: A. Chiarelli: '"L'Incoronazione di Poppea' ò 'Il Nerone"' in *RIM* IX (1974), pp.117–151.

43. ASV, Procuratori di S. Marco, Procuratoria Chiesa, b.91, proc.207, f.41v.

44. *Motetti a voce sola di diversi Eccelentissimi Autori* (Venice, 1645). The other composers represented were Monteverdi, G. Casati, N. Fontei, G.B. Trevisi, P. Tamburini and G. Filippi.

45. *Madrigali Concertati a due, tre e quattro voci Libro Terzo del Signor Gio: Rovetta Maestro di Capella della Serenissima Republica, raccolti da Gio: Battista Volpe e dedicati al Molto Illustre Signor, e Padron mio osser.mo il Sig. Francesco Cavalli Organista di S. Marco* (Venice, Vincenti, 1645).

46. See Appendix III/ii for extracts from the dedication.

47. ASV, Reg. Monialium Arch. Curia Patriarcale.

48. ASV, S. Lorenzo, b.24, V.

49. *ibid.*, Q, ff.8–9. Document dated 24th July, 1642.

50. See: L. Schrade: *Monteverdi: Creator of Modern Music* (London, Gollancz, 1951), p.360.

51. ASV, S. Lorenzo, b.24, B, f.24.

52. *ibid.*, f.7. This property was to become a source of trouble for Cavalli. He rented it out to a Signor B. Negrini in 1647. In the 1660's there was a prolonged legal procedure between Cavalli and Negrini for non-payment of rent (*ibid.*, b.24, T). Cavalli's case was handled by Minato.

53. ASV, S. Lorenzo, b.23, 21. Claudia died on 30 June 1645 (f.33v). Her will, dated 16 January 1645, left everything to her husband, and survives in two copies, one of which is made by Cavalli himself. Bianca died on 1 April 1646 (f.33v). Maria's penultimate will is in ff.23–4v.

54. ASV, Provveditori alla sanità, Necrologio, b.877 (1651).

55. ASV, S. Lorenzo, b.24, DD. This document states that her last will was published on 16 September. The Necrologio records for the years 1652–1655 are missing in the Venice Archivio di Stato.

56. ASV, Notarile Claudio Paulini, Testamenti, b.799, f.381.

57. In Cavalli's own will, over 20 years later, he made a similar bequest to his servant Maddalena from Crema. See below.

58. See Appendix III/iii for the relevant quotation from Maria Sosomeno's will.

59. ASV, S. Lorenzo, b.24, BB, f.23, for example, is a document dated 19 December 1652 in which Cavalli transferred 400 ducats to Barbieri.

60. In the inventory of 'scritture' made at Cavalli's death is a receipt (ASV, S. Lorenzo, b.24, 16) dated 12 May 1671, for 133 ducats which Cavalli loaned to Giulio Alberghini, Maria's step-brother.
61. ASV, Scuola Grande di S. Marco, b.194, f.179. For the Teatro Sant' Apollinare, see my D.Phil. thesis: *The Teatro Sant' Apollinare and the development of seventeenth-century Venetian opera* (Oxford, 1975).
62. See: B. Brunelli: 'L'impresario in angustie' in *RID* III (1941), pp.311–341.
63. See: N. Pirrotta: 'Il caval zoppo . . .', *op. cit.*
64. Strozzi published his libretto under the anagrammatical pseudonym of Luigi Zorzisto. *Veremonda* was a reworking of Cicognini's *Celio,* performed in Florence in 1646. See:
L. Bianconi and T. Walker: 'Dalla *Finta Pazza* . . .', *op. cit.*
65. *ibid.*
66. See L Bianconi: 'Caletti' in *Dizionario Biografico degli Italiani* XVI (1973), pp.691–692.
67. ASV, Scuola Grande di S. Marco, b.188, f.14. See Appendix III/iv for the complete text of Cavalli's letter.
68. *ibid.*, b.194, f.73. Contract dated 5 May 1657.
69. *ibid.*, b.194, f.266.
70. ASV, Procuratori di S. Marco, Procuratia Chiesa, b.91, proc.207, f.41v.
71. ASV, S. Lorenzo, b.24, BB. f.30.
72. *ibid.*, f.35. Document dated 17 February 1656.
73. *ibid.*, f.47. (In the preface to his libretto *Orimonte,* Minato stated: 'Sappi, ch'io non fò del Poeta. Le mie applicationi sono nel Foro . . .').
74. *Musiche Sacre concernenti Messa e Salmi Concertati con Istromenti Imni Antifone e Sonate, a Due, 3, 4, 5, 6, 8, 10, e 12 Voci, di Francesco Cavalli, Organista della Serenissima Republica in S. Marco* (Venice, Vincenti, 1656).
75. See Appendix III/v for the preface.
76. ASV, S. Lorenzo, b.24, S (83).
77. See Appendix I for list of revivals.
78. See: H. Prunières: *L'opéra italien en France avant Lulli* (Paris, 1913), pp.213ff.
79. Paris, B.N., Ministère des Affaires Etrangères, *Rome* 137, f.263. Quoted in Prunières, *op. cit.*, pp.393–394. See Appendix III/vi for the text.
80. *ibid., France* 281, f.442. Quoted in Prunières, *op. cit.*, p.400.
81. ASV, Procuratori di S. Marco, Procuratia de supra, fasc.35: Decreti e terminazioni, reg.146, f.75v.
82. *ibid.* See Appendix III/vii for the Procurators' declaration.
83. *ibid.*, f.76v.
84. ASV, S Lorenzo, b.23, f.13 is a document written after Cavalli's

death, in which, among other claims for money made from Cavalli's estate, is one on behalf of the late 'Giacomo da Muran fu Giovan del detto qm Signor Cavalli e si condusse seco in Francia'. The money claim was for unpaid expenses incurred in France. The document is backdated by 13 years to 22 September 1662.

85. ASV, S. Lorenzo, b.24, BB, f.54 is a long document dated 18 August 1661,wherein two large areas of Gambarare land are being rented out. The document is signed by Paulini on behalf of Cavalli:

'Io Claudio Paulini Nodaro sottoscritto per nome et ordine del sudetto S. Cavalli che si trova al presente in Francia al Servitio di quella Maesta con permissione e licenza dell'Eccmo Senato.'

86. The 1671 revision of Doglioni's *Cosa notabile*, p.207, states that Cavalli was received at the Bavarian court as well as that of France:

'. . . per le sue dilettevoli Compositioni fù chiamato alla Corte di Francia; alla Corte di Baviera dove diede gran saggi della sua virtù'

87. Quoted in Caffi, *op. cit.*, p.280.

88. ASV, Scuola Grande di S. Marco, b.188, f.380. The document is badly damaged. See Appendix III/viii for a transcription.

89. *ibid.*, b.194, f.49 is a letter to Marco Faustini, missing both date and signature, but not written by Cavalli. The writer states, on behalf of Cavalli, that 'non servendogli il tempo in riguardo delle molte occupationi de' suoi interessi, assai per la sua absenza fin hora sconvolti.'

90. ASV, Scuola Grande di S. Marco, b.194, f.50 is a contract signed by both Cavalli and Faustini.

91. These facts are learned from a letter of Pietro Dolfin to the Duke of Braunschweig, now in the Niedersachs Staatsarchiv in Hanover. I am grateful to Thomas Walker for supplying me with this information.

92. See Chapter 3, below.

93. 'Compongo sole all'horo che ma ne prende la fantasia, e sono si poco resistente alla fatica, che, se un hora di più del mio uso m'affatico, sono subito amalato'. (Nowadays I compose only when I feel moved to do so; and I have so little resistance to fatigue that, if I work for an hour longer than I am used to, I become ill.)

94. ASV, S. Lorenzo, b.23, 13: a claim from the solicitor Signor Fausto Negri, dated 1 August, 1676, It alleges that Cavalli employed his father, Signor Carlo Negri, as a lawyer from 22 September 1662, but failed to pay him during his thirteen years' service.

95. ASV, Procuratori di S. Marco, Procuatia de supra, fasc.35: Decreti e terminazioni, reg.146, f.144v.

96. *ibid.*, f.149v. See:

E. Selfridge-Field: *Venetian Instrumental Music* (Oxford, 1975), Appendix F, pp.297–308.

97. See: D. Arnold: 'Cavalli at St. Mark's' in *Early Music* IV.3 (1976),

pp.266–274.

98. ASV, S. Lorenzo, b.24, DD, refs. I.4, C.2, I.5, I.6; BB, f.57.

99. ASV, S. Lorenzo, b.23, 21, ff.15–15v.

100. ASV, Notarile Claudio Paulini, Testamenti, b.488, f.206.

101. ASV, Provveditori alla sanità, Necrologio 886 (1676).

102. See Caffi *op. cit.*, pp.55–56.

103. ASV, Procuratori di S. Marco, Procuratia de supra, fasc.35: Decreti e terminazioni, reg.147, f.29.

104. Published, with some slight errors, by Wiel in 'Francesco Cavalli . . .', *op. cit.*

105. Cavalli had attempted to withdraw himself from the problems attached to the Crema property when his father had died in 1642 (see p.2 above). But his possession of these properties in 1676 indicates that they eventually came to him on the death of his sisters.

106. In earlier documents Signor Medici's name has been given as Faustineo (ASV, S. Lorenzo, b.24, V). While it is most likely that he possessed and used to names, it is also conceivable that Diambra Caterina consecutively married two members of the same family.

107. ASV, S. Lorenzo, b.24, CC, f.27.

108. *ibid.*, b.24, BB, f.61.

109. *ibid.*, b.24, CC, f.24.

110. *ibid.*, b.24, CC, f.30.

111. *ibid.*, b.23, f.16.

CHAPTER II

Libretto

Before examining the music of Cavalli's operas, it is first necessary to consider the state of opera at the beginning of the period. Since the musical matter was obviously much influenced by the character and style of the libretto upon which it was based, a study of the libretto itself, and of its formation and development, is a useful starting point.[1] For the libretto reflected current audience tastes, and can therefore serve as a measure of general operatic development.

The earliest operatic ventures, written and performed by members of the Florentine *Camerata* at the turn of the century, were without exception based upon mythological themes. Of these, two in particular (those of Daphne and Orpheus) captured the imagination of both creators and audiences, and the earliest operas regularly reverted to them.[2] The legend of Apollo and Daphne had had a notable setting in the 1589 celebrations of the marriage between Ferdinando de' Medici and Christine de Lorraine, when it was performed as the third *intermedio* in Bargagli's *La Pellegrina.*[3] The poet Rinuccini, later a prominent member of the *Camerata*, was present and participant at these celebrations (as indeed were such notable composers as Peri, Caccini and Cavalieri). *Dafne,* his own version of the legend, was set several times by the earliest opera composers such as Peri in 1598, Gagliano in 1608 and later Schütz in 1627.[4] In 1640, Busenello wrote another version, *Gli Amori d'Apollo e di Dafne.* Similarly the legend of Orpheus and Eurydice was introduced into opera by Rinuccini, whose libretto *Euridice* was set by Peri and also by Caccini in 1600. Alessandro

Striggio reworked it as *Orfeo* for Monteverdi in Mantua in 1607. Later librettists also seized upon the legend: Buti for Rossi's *Orfeo* in 1647, and Aureli for Sartorio's *Orfeo* of 1673.[5] Other mythological stories followed, such as *Aretusa* by Corsini, set by Vitali in 1620, Tronsarellis *La Catena d'Adone*, set by Mazzocchi in 1626 (based on Marini's celebrated and contentious poem), and the first opera performed in a Venetian public theatre, Ferrari's *Andromeda*.

This strong mythological trend was accompanied by a gradual move towards an *opera buffa* style in Rome.[6] The introduction of comic characters such as servants, the speeding-up of plots and the creating of quasi-farcial situations was in the first place an almost direct result of three visits to Spain by the poet Rospigliosi, later Pope Clement IX.[7] As a representative of the Vatican he spent considerable periods in Madrid between 1625 and 1653, the third lasting for a decade between 1643 and 1653 when he returned with the Barbarinis from their Parisian exile. While in Spain he was strongly influenced by the playwrights Calderòn and Lope de Vega, and he became familiar with the type of *comedia de capa y espada* which so influenced the eventual *opera buffa*. Such dramatic concepts were by no means foreign to Italians, for they had been an integral feature of Italian theatre for several centuries. The comic element in early opera was part of a long-standing theatrical tradition which went back to the ancient Roman comedies of Plautus and Terence, and proceeded through the works of Ariosto and the *commedia dell'arte* to the plays of Goldoni and Metastasio. Thus when music-drama reached Venice in 1637 it was to be expected that plots would be mythologically based, with elements of comedy creeping in, as was indeed happening in Rome at this time.

Contrary to current practice in Rome and Florence, public opera in Venice was not an individual performance for a particular festivity, such as the celebration of a marriage or the welcoming of distinguished visitors. Venice had in the past presented some occasional pieces, such as the lost *Proserpina rapita* by Strozzi and Monteverdi, performed in the Mocenigo palace in 1630. But now operas were shown repeatedly, with plots unrelated to any specific occasion. So there was an immediate and important difference in libretto construction. The Roman five-act formula, with its Prologue and Epilogue saluting its patrons or guests and abundant opportunity for intermediary divisions such as ballos, was invalid in a new context where audiences went to the theatre simply for entertainment. Stories began to be told in three acts. Prologues, if they existed at all, were considerably curtailed, and bore some relation to the plot without trying to involve any member of the audience. Epilogues vanished almost completely, as did elaborate ensemble finales. Librettists took care to end the opera happily, even if this involved considerable alteration of narratives. Such changes were made very self-consciously by the librettists themselves. Busenello, for example, who altered the historical ending of his *Didone* so that she did not die but married Iarbas, thought it necessary to defend this and other changes with the general statement that 'poets are licensed to alter not only Fiction but also History'.[8] For the audiences, who went to the opera in the 1640's and 1650's in much the same spirit as cinema audiences in the 1940's and 1950's, were constantly to be courted, pleased and above all entertained.

Of the first generation of Venetian librettists, Francesco Busenello was himself the individual who stands out most clearly, and whose career reflects early developments in libretto-writing.[9] An intellectual who had studied at Padua, he was well acquainted with classical and mythological literature. Not unlike the early *Camerata*, or Cardinal Rospigliosi in Rome, for him writing for the theatre was a kind of intellectual pastime. Five of his liberettos were set to music: *Gli Amori d'Apollo e di Dafne, Didone, Giulio Cesare*[10] and *Statira* were all set by Cavalli. *L'Incoronazione di Poppea* was set by Monteverdi in 1642. All these texts were published in a collected edition of his dramatic works in 1656 in Venice, and this was a curious exception to the standard practice whereby librettos were published to coincide with their theatrical performances.

Even within the first three years of Busenello's performed works, the style and form of the libretto changed greatly. *Apollo e Dafne* is a loosely constructed poem in three acts. Although it specifies separate scenes, the action still seems merely dissected into convenient portions, which appear as a series of consecutive tableaux rather than as a continuous unfolding drama. A character seldom appears in two consecutive scenes. Yet within this loose framework there is a pristine purity and lyricism. Following the principles of the *Camerata*, the music heightens the effect of the poetry, which itself is contemplative and protracted, with little fast-moving action. Cavalli's setting is one of his earliest extant operas and is a revealing document, but the poem could exist on its own without music. The serenity of Busenello's text struck a poetic vein in libretto-writing which was very rarely achieved thereafter. In the Prologue, for example, Sonno sings:

Questa è l'hora felice
Da me più favorita,
In cui godo vedere
Dentr' un dormir profondo,
La Natura sopita.
Poco lungi è la Diva
Che sparge a man profusa humide perle.
Poco lungi è la luce
Che per sentier dorato il dì conduce.

Apollo e Dafne also shows a distinct echo of the pastoral era (it contains a *ballo di ninfe e pastori* in I.4), and such characterisation as exists is pale and uniform. The strength of the mythological ancestry is obviously reflected in the subject of the work, but even here its dissolution begins to be apparent. The Prologue includes a *ballo dei fantasmi*, foreshadowing a concentration on the supernatural that was shortly to eclipse mythological interest.

Didone appeared only a year after *Apollo e Dafne*, but already there is a vast difference between the two librettos. Scenes are organised in logical sequences which severally constitute a dramatic entity, and there is a marked coherence and fluency conspicuously absent in the previous work. A possible reason for this is that Busenello was now dealing with characters mortal (albeit mythological) rather than immortal, and their story was more immediately presentable than the somewhat ethereal accidents of Apollo and Daphne. From retrospective consideration, *Didone*'s construction is still highly unusual. Curiously like Berlioz's structure, the first act is devoted to the fall of Troy, principally to account for Aeneas' flight from it, but also to include the tragedy of Cassandra. This means that Dido herself does not appear until the second act, and that the main story, with Dido, Aeneas and Iarbas, is confined to the last two acts.

L'Incoronazione di Poppea, following *Didone* a year later, develops what might be termed the impurities that *Didone* introduced. Basically a story of the conflict between passion and reason, any high moral tone, such as that previously shown by Eurydice or Daphne, is completely abandoned. Nero and Poppaea overcome all obstacles to fulfilment of their lustful relationship. Ironically this one development perhaps impedes another: that of credible characterisation. When, for example, Nero murders Seneca, persecutes Octavia, ruins the marriage between Otho and Drusilla, and yet manages to remain the 'hero' with the concluding love duet, psychological coherence seems highly questionable. But *Didone* and *Poppea* both make greater use of servant characters, to provide comic interludes and so to relieve tension. The *valletto* and *damigella* in *Poppea* are among the earliest examples of young servant lovers at the courts of the rich and potentially tragic, and it is they who provide contrast, for example immediately after Seneca's death. The three *damigelle* in *Didone*—splendid character sketches of court gossips—do the same after the first meeting between Dido and Aeneas.

Poetically, Busenello's keen grasp of dramatic situation provides a lively and well-modulated text. Given that the clash between passion and reason is the principle upon which *Poppea* is based, one of the early climaxes is the meeting and argument between Nero and Seneca as representatives of the two sides (I.9), from which the following extract is taken:

NERONE: Tu mi sforzi allo sdegno; al tuo dispetto,
E del popolo in onta, e del Senato,
E d'Ottavia, e del Cielo, e dell'abisso,
Siansi giuste, od ingiuste le mie voglie,
Hoggi, hoggi Poppea sarà mia moglie.

SENECA: Siano innocenti i Regi,
O s'aggravano sol di colpe illustri;
S'innocenza si perde
Perdasi sol per guadagnare i Regni,
Che il peccato commesso
Per aggrandir l'Impero
Si assolve da se stesso;
Ma che una femminella habbia possanza
Di condurti agli errori,
Non è colpa di Rege, e Semideo.
E un misfatto plebeo.

Nero's initial arrogance and confidence has been gradually broken down into these short, detached phrases, loaded with repetitions, both of word ('*e* d'Ottavia, *e* del Cielo, *e* dell'abisso'; '*hoggi, hoggi* Poppea sarà mia moglie') and of sound ('siansi *giuste* od *ingiuste* le mie voglie'). The effect is therefore one of childish petulance and lack of control. By complete contrast, Seneca's well-measured and regular lines, particularly featuring long vowel-sounds, and their gentle elisions, give him quiet and calm dignity; and the force of his final line, where he directs at Nero the full realistic weight of his reasoned accusations, is all the more devastating after the quiet control of its build-up.

So the early 1640's were a period of changing concepts. Busenello's later librettos, *Giulio Cesare* and *Statira,* show a rather less positive sense of direction. There is some doubt as to the dating of *Giulio Cesare.* Ivanovich, in his *Memorie teatrali,*[11] gives 1646, but the libretto did not appear until 1656 when all Busenello's librettos were published for the first time. By now he was in the last years of his life (he died in 1659, aged 61), and in many ways *Giulio Cesare* does seem the work of a man at the end of his career, going very much his own way, and even departing from the traditions which he himself had set up. It reverts to a five-act structure, now rare, and brings back the Epilogue, which salutes not only the Grimani family (in whose theatre, SS Giovanni e Paolo, the work was performed) but also the people of Venice:

NETTUNO: Libertà senti, ascolta
Fatidico Nettun cio che predice
Di qua à secoli molti,
Tu canterai le lodi, & io gl'applausi
Di VENETIA immortal in stil giocondo
Nel TEATRO GRIMAN famoso al Mondo.

CHORO: Viva VENETIA viva,
Ogni penna descriva
Del suo nome le glorie
De suoi gesti l'historie
Et il Destino ingemmi le Corone
Al suo generosissimo LEONE.

As in the *Didone* preface, Busenello seeks, albeit pedantically, to justify his changes to his reader:

> If there are five acts and not three, you must remember that all ancient Dramas and particularly the tragedies of Seneca, are distributed in five acts. The changes of location should not seem strange, for a writer must obey his whim. . . . Remember always how Tacitus praised Seneca, saying that he had a genius adaptable to the tastes of his time.[12]

Perhaps this preoccupation with the ancient writers coincides with the current popularity among Venetians of drawing comparisons between ancient Rome and contemporary Venice. During the 1650's in particular, Venice was politically in some considerable distress, and one method of escape was to hark back to the former glories of the city, which were apparently comparable only with the most illustrious of previous civilisations. Ivanovich's *Minerva al Tavolino* (1681)[13] devotes two entire chapters to the subject:

1. *La Republica di Venezia imitando la Grandezza della Romana, rinovo la magnificenza de' Teatri.*

4. *De' Teatri Romani, e della differenza, che v̓' tràquelli, e questi di Venezia.*

Giulio Cesare does in many ways seem more akin to the splendid courtly celebrations of Florence or Rome, with its unusual structure and a cast of thirty-four. Yet the fact that Venice and the Grimanis are specifically cited in the Epilogue manifestly establishes that it was written for the Venetian theatre, and as the score does not survive it remains a puzzle for the present-day historian. Incidentally, it is perhaps interesting to observe how Busenello treats Caesar's famous 'Et tu, Brute?':

> Ah sacrileghi, ah mostri, ah parracidi,
> E sei tu Bruto ancora, e sei tu figlio
> Complice auttor del mio mortal periglio?

This moving section of recitative is unfortunately followed by a three-stanza aria for Caesar before he dies, which would again suggest that the opera was later than 1646, for at that time the passion for arias had by no means begun to disrupt dramatic situation in this way.

Statira of 1656 is very much a product of its time. Here

Busenello presents a complex plot in what had by now emerged as the Faustini tradition, with two pairs of princely lovers enduring extremely entangled situations before achieving their desires. He has taken a story that is again basically historical, but altered it for the theatre in the current manner. Despite such an obvious effort to adapt it to present-day tastes, Busenello's libretto did not serve the composer as fluently as did those of most contemporary writers, and Cavalli had to alter the text considerably when setting it. Even the structure of individual scenes had to be altered, for example Act I, 5, a solo comic scene for Vaffrino. Here Busenello has set out the text as a four-stanza aria (with each stanza consisting of four eight-syllable lines and two of eleven syllables) and five lines of recitative. Cavalli had two attempts at setting this scene, each one retaining the character Ermosilla for the previous scene. First, he began with a recitative for Ermosilla and followed this with a setting of one stanza only from the aria text for Vaffrino, with a ritornello. Three of the five lines of recitative were then set, and the ritornello for the following scene was begun. On second thoughts, Cavalli crossed all this out, and with the help of a colleague or pupil[14] who recopied these existing sections, began again, this time adding a complete aria for Ermosilla (with a text that does not appear at all in Busenello's libretto) before Vaffrino's own aria. Both ways, Cavalli felt obliged to restructure Busenello's existing plan in order to make it acceptable.

Busenello was nonetheless the writer who firmly laid the foundations of the Venetian libretto at the beginning of the 1640's; and despite the fact that he himself preferred to depart from these foundations in the latter years of his life, his librettos remain the bequest of a sensitive and humorous poet.[15]

The next librettist in whose works the opera form developed and settled was Giovanni Faustini.[16] His first libretto *La Virtù de' strali d'Amore* was set by Cavalli in 1642, and before his early death in 1651 ten more appeared. After 1651 four of his works were set posthumously. Very little is known about Faustini himself. Even the date of his birth is in some doubt. The necrology records of his parish San Vidal state that he was 36 when he died.[17] This conflicts however with the libretto of his *Alciade* (performed in 1667) whose preface (probably written by his brother Marco) gives his age in 1651 as 31: 'Death took him prematurely in 1651, the thirty-second year of his life'.[18] (It is probably safer to trust his brother's accuracy than that of the Necrology records.)[19] Certainly Faustini's situation was very different from those of both his predecessor Busenello and his successors Minato and Aureli, all of whom were professional men who cultivated literary pursuits for amusement and diversion. Faustini was compelled to try and manage an opera house in order to straighten his finances, and his libretto output as a whole shows signs of a somewhat phrenetic attitude to the completion of his works.

The period of Faustini's libretto-writing, between 1642 and 1651, was also that of the standardising of the Venetian libretto formula. Faustini collaborated almost solely with Cavalli in this decade, so that the close working relationship between these two men was a powerful factor in determining the direction of the libretto. The three-act structure was finally consolidated, with the first act introducing all the main characters and exposing the main dramatic threads; the second act developing and entangling these elements; and the third act finally resolving them. Within individual acts Faustini at his best produced structures of contrasting sections, where the deployment of supernatural or other minor characters was masterly. The first act of *Rosinda* is a model of a close tripartite structure. It opens with the main character Nerea asking assistance of her fellow sorcerers in the winning back of her lover Clitofonte; they advise her to seek the help of Pluto and Persephone. The second sequence introduces Rosinda and Clitofonte and the servant Rudione, who at the exit of Rosinda and Clitofonte has a comic encounter with the fourth lover Thisandro and is left alone on stage to tell the audience about his fear and hunger. The act ends with a prolonged sequence in the Underworld, where Nerea's plea is heard by Pluto and Persephone who promise her their assistance. Supernatural characters were often used by Faustini to close first acts in this way, however relevant or irrelevant might be their participation in the action. *La Virtù de' strali d'Amore, Egisto, Doriclea* and *Oristeo* all close their first acts with gods or mythological figures, who introduce a small ballo constituting a kind of punctuation mark to close the act. This seems an obvious residuum from the era of the mythological plot, where the acts were also concluded in as spectacular a way as possible.

A particular feature of Faustini's librettos, adopted also by his successors, is the often lengthy introduction to the story, printed at the front of each libretto. With Faustini, this scene- and context-setting prelude, often spanning many years and embracing several geographical locations, grew to what seem like excessive proportions in, for example, *Eritrea* (1652) where it occupies over four closely-printed pages of libretto. That to Aureli's subsequent *Erismena* (1656) similarly occupies three pages. The presence of these *antefatti* can perhaps be explained by the fact that the printed librettos were sold both in the theatres' foyers and in bookshops elsewhere in Venice, and were probably therefore bought by a large proportion of the audience. A keen opera-goer would read this prelude, and thus at the start of the actual performance he would already have some familiarity with the characters and their motivations, and a great desire to know how the complex entanglements of the story would be resolved. It is just possible to understand the operas without familiarising oneself with their prefaces; but there were distinct psychological advantages in having prepared a certain proportion of the audience for immediate involvement with the action.

Faustini's librettos all begin powerfully. The first acts show a strength and coherence of construction that seems to promise a neatly-shaped whole. It is unfortunately here that his hurry in libretto-writing is apparent. The second acts rarely, and the third acts never, live up to the strong starts. Second acts, with complex plot entanglement, need to be tightly and thoughtfully constructed in order best to convey the complexities in a coherent form. But frequently they are overloaded with irrelevant scenes and comic contrasts which are as long as, if not longer than, the serious passages they must relieve. The third acts similarly seem to lose all shape and design. They hurtle precipitately towards a denouement, which often seems bathetic, inconsequential and therefore unsatisfactory. *La Virtù de' strali d'Amore* is an example of this. Act III, which should ideally be as short as possible to conclude the events, is in this case as long as the first two acts put together, and its utterly variegated sections (there are seven separate subdivisions, as opposed to four in the first act) lose all coherence.

Egisto's structure similarly loses tauntness throughout its course. Act I is in two neat sections. Act II begins with a long sequence for the serious characters, relieved by a comic solo scene, and ends with gods. The third act all takes place in one location, but with no fewer than five separate sections, resulting in a haphazard structure that is hardly satisfactory at this stage of the opera. It would therefore appear that external pressures and anxieties distracted Faustini to the extent that his works often lost dramatic impetus and fizzled out towards the end.

Before Faustini, Busenello had drawn chiefly upon mythological stories for his plots, and later in the 1650's and 1660's historical subjects were to be exploited by Minato. In further contrast to his predecessors and successors, Faustini employed neither of these sources, but as a rule produced original stories. There are of course exceptions. *Calisto* and *Titone* are both mythologically based. *Doriclea* is set in a conflict between the Medes and Armenians, which became a regular feature of some of the later historical librettos, like Minato's *Orimonte* (1650), Sorrentino's *Ciro* (1654) and Aureli's *Erismena* (1656). Certainly individual mythological characters were retained in Prologues, but usually they were recognisable deities, such as Pluto, Persephone, Mercury, Jove, Mars and so on.

Faustini's plots are all in the same mould. They all centre round two or three pairs of princely lovers, who are coupled and uncoupled throughout the action. Their characters are superficially presented with little difference between them. But the text of individual speeches (that is, arias) does allow for thought-progression, so providing scope for character development. The actions of these main characters are always love-motivated, and the situations in which they find themselves usually bizarre. They are supported by their servants: generally two or three to one of the main characters, and with a pair of young lovers among them. They often include a Leporello-type comic manservant, and other stock characters of distinct *commedia dell'arte* derivation, such as elderly fathers and aged nurses; and finally the gods. It was a pattern which rarely altered and never failed. The differences between librettos are therefore in situation and event, not in outline or format.

Interest in magic and the supernatural increased enormously during Faustini's literary reign. His first opera, *La Virtù de' strali d'Amore,* already has strong inclinations towards it, with one stage set described in the libretto as 'Selva horrida incantata' (I.16), and the first act ending with a 'Ballo delle Maghe'. Similarly *Ormindo* includes a fortune-telling episode. The plot of *Rosinda* hinges entirely on two of the four lovers drinking from a magic fountain, the effect of which is only annulled by the application of another potion. *Eritrea*'s complex plot is only solved when a case of child-swapping and disguise is revealed. Disguise and baby-swapping were standard methods of achieving complexity in librettos, to which magic itself was a short cut. The element of disguise, which had also appeared in Faustini's first libretto (*La Virtù,* where Erabena is disguised as Eumete, a valet) persisted strongly in the 1650's, when indeed it was one of the most characteristic features. The first works of both Minato and Aureli, the most notable and successful of the next generation of librettists, each include disguise. Minato's *Orimonte* (1650, set by Cavalli) is based on a case of baby-swapping; Aureli's *Erginda* (1652, set by Sartorio), like his subsequent *Erismena,* has its heroine disguised as a man almost throughout. Right through the 1650's, librettos which were original, not based on mythology or history, always centred on at least one character, and very often two, being in disguise. Besides those already mentioned there were *Oristeo* (1651, Cavalli-Faustini), *Eritrea* (1652, Cavalli-Faustini), *Veremonda* (1653, Cavalli-Strozzi), *Ciro* (1654, Cavalli-Sorrentino, with no fewer than four disguises), *Statira* (1656, Cavalli-Busenello), *Artemisia* (1657, Cavalli-Minato) and *Le Fortune di Rodope e di Damira* (1657, Ziani-Aureli). Even in the mythology-based *Calisto* (1651, Cavalli-Faustini), Jove disguises himself as Diana in order to pursue Callisto more closely, and this feature may have been the reason for the choice of such a subject.

Faustini's librettos, then, were becoming much more geared to the dramatic, the theatrical and the complex. The increases and advances were obviously to be balanced by certain losses, and in this case it was perhaps the poetry which suffered. The libretto text, as correctly seen by Faustini, was simply a basis for a musico-theatrical event, not a literary work in its own right. Rarely therefore did he achieve poetical heights comparable with those of Busenello. His texts always required the added dimension of the music for which they were written. Technically they followed the standard format of the seventeenth century and set out the text in lines of seven or eleven syllables. These lengths were employed interchangeably for recitative. In addition to these, there were lines of four, five, six or eight syllables, which generally implied aria verse. Faustini was thus imposing some sort of musico-poetic structure on the composer. Whether or not the composer took any notice of such guidelines was a different matter, and certainly

Cavalli preferred to treat the text in his own way, taking arias from recitative lines and vice versa. Nonetheless Faustini had a clear idea of where in a scene the action should be, and where it should be halted temporarily for a period of contemplation, reflection or greater revelation of emotion.

Faustini's libretto-writing was curtailed by his premature death, but his contribution to the medium during the 1640's was vitally important for its development. He was highly esteemed by his contemporaries and also by his successors, although their praise of him could have been coloured by standard pathos due to one cut short in his prime, or even perhaps made in the gratifying knowledge that a potential competitor was safely dead. Two more of his librettos were set posthumously before the end of the decade: *Eupatra* in 1655 and *Elena* in 1659. *Elena* was in fact left unfinished by Faustini, and it was completed for performance by Minato, by now a well-established librettist in his own right. Faustini's work probably only amounted to the overall structure and scene-casting, with none of the actual text having been written. Minato, a highly organised writer, always manipulated his acts to include exactly 20 scenes each, and as *Elena* does not conform to this pattern it is reasonable to suppose that it was Faustini's structure and Minato's text. In the preface, Minato was generous in saluting his dead colleague:

> The subject of this Drama came from the great genius of the late Giovanni Faustini, of famous memory; whose virtue astounded the theatres not only in this city, but also those in the farthest regions. Many famous writers were asked, after his death, to complete this work by writing the text, and for various reasons they all refused. I have not been able to turn down such an honour, and although my own defects as a poet disturb me as I make this resolution, I am comforted by the knowledge that these failings were shown in Xerse, Artemisia and Antioco, which were my own subjects, whereas here I shall be better tolerated, for I have as a basis for my work this subject of a very famous Virtuoso.
>
> I pray to Heaven that the peace of his remains will not be disturbed by whatever of my imperfections damages his own merits. Let me make it clear that whatever there is that is bad is by me, and all that is good is by him. You, courteous reader,

> admire the subject, and have pity on the text: and live happily.[20]

Much later, in the 1660's, there was a further revival of interest in Faustini's librettos at the Teatro SS Giovanni e Paolo, doubtless due to the fact that Marco Faustini was now running this theatre. In 1665 Marco tried to initiate this revival by asking Ziani to set *Doriclea.* Ziani agreed to do so, but complained that the poetry was rather old-fashioned for the time.[21] The rival of *Orontea* (Cesti-Cicognini) in the following year included the new prologue from *Doriclea. Alciade* (set by Ziani) appeared in 1667, and *Meraspe* (set by Pallavicino) in 1668. The preface to *Alciade* (surely written by Marco Faustini) is a glorious eulogy of Giovanni Faustini's life:

> Giovanni Faustini, at an age too young for proper enjoyment, applied his genius to music-dramas, in which he excelled above all at invention. Therefore during the course of only nine years (for he died suddenly in 1651, aged only 31) the theatres of this city presented, to great applause, La Virtù de' strali d'Amore, Egisto, Ormindo, Titone, Doriclea, Ersilda, Euripo, Oristeo, Rosinda, Calisto, Eritrea, and after his death, Eupatra then Elena rapita da Teseo, clothed with the verse of a sublime Virtuoso; all set to music either by the singular virtue of Francesco Cavalli, a most honoured organist in the most Serene Republic; or Pietro Andrea Ziana, now maestro di cappella in Vienna. They met not only the joy and satisfaction of this city, which hears so many similar productions, but also those in many other major cities of Italy, where they were heard increasingly often with every amount of applause; indeed his many inventions have often met with more than one musical setting.[22]

At the end of the Prologue there is a further note to the reader, presumably printed there because it was a last-minute insertion. It informs the reader that two complete scenes and certain passages in two further scenes are being omitted in performance. It is interesting that, out of deference to the dead librettist, the whole of his original text was printed, but that the scenes which in the 1660's were now not workable or desirable were axed. In Faustini's lifetime any libretto changes introduced during the rehearsal period were probably also altered in the printed text. Similar problems of using old librettos in the 1660's can also be inferred from the *Meraspe* publication (which incidentally refers to Faustini as 'il Sofocle delle Scene, e l'Euripide de' theatri moderni . . .'). The preface reads:

> The present Drama was left incomplete by Giovanni Faustini, who had written two acts, with ariettas, but mostly in *stile recitativo,* as was the custom in his day. To adapt it to current taste, it has been necessary to make certain changes, but without altering at all the subject or the scenario, left in all perfection by the author, as was the Prologue. . . .
>
> For the sake of brevity we do not perform the verses marked in the margin with commas. But you can still read them for greater comprehension of the Drama.
>
> Be sympathetic to certain printing errors, a result of haste.[23]

Last-minute changes are again implied by the last sentence. No further librettos by Giovanni Faustini were attempted, and it seems likely that, as Ziani had observed, his style of 'puro romanzo' with monsters, gods and the supernatural, was well and truly outdated.

Resti dunque quel birbon
Con Proserpina e Pluton.

By the beginning of the 1650's, then, the shape of the libretto was firmly established in three acts, with an increasing emphasis on disguise and complexity, and with the aria emerging in a delineated closed form. The ensuing decade was one of subtle refinement. It was a period of thinning out, both musically and textually, so that plots involved fewer characters.[24] Conversely, the already marked element of complexity was increased, producing plots that required the audience to keep fully alert in order to understand them. It must be remembered that, however complex and unfathomable such librettos as *Ciro* and *Statira* may appear to the twentieth-century historian, seventeenth-century audiences had been conditioned to them by over a decade's experience. It was a self-generating process: the more complex the plots, the more the comprehension and concentration of the audiences were taxed. Once they had mastered a plot with perhaps two disguises, it was necessary to add a third disguise lest they became too familiar with, and therefore bored by, the present format. The function of opera was still to entertain the audience, whatever device was necessary.

In 1649, Venice had seen the first performances of two operas by the librettist Giacinto Andrea Cicognini: *Giasone* (set by Cavalli) and *Orontea* (set by Cesti). These two works were the most outstandingly successful in the whole of the seventeenth century, for they were revived repeatedly all over Italy. Cicognini was essentially a playwright who ventured only four times into the opera house, but the resounding triumph of *Giasone* and *Orontea* confirms his position among the foremost librettists of his day. The taut dramatic construction of his dramas suggests that his intimate knowledge of the theatre was crucial to his approach to opera. He could furnish his librettos with ideal proportions of serious situations and comedy, and so provide the essential contrasts.

The 1650's hailed the new generation of librettists. Aurelio Aureli[25] and Nicolo Minato[26] (both members of the Accademia degli Imperfetti) had their first works performed early in the decade, and by the 1660's they were fully established as successful and popular writers. Both these men, like their contemporary composers Cesti, Ziani and Draghi, established themselves in Venetian theatres and then travelled elsewhere to employment at courts. Minato went to Austria, Aureli to Parma, so spreading the operatic medium and their own reputations. (This is again in contrast to Faustini, who apparently never worked outside Venice.) It is interesting that, less than twenty years after the advent of public opera, the creators of it were moving back to the constant attraction of court presentations. Artists seemed to appreciate the luxurious splendour of court life (despite the hard work entailed), and, although some of them periodically returned to work in Venice, they tended to settle in these grander surroundings. Both Aureli and Minato had been accustomed, by their upbringing, to a higher standard of living than that of Faustini. Minato himself was a nobleman and a lawyer, and his first librettos appeared very intermittently, with gaps of two or more years between them. *Orimonte* was performed in 1650, *Xerse* in 1655, *Artemisia* in 1657, *Antioco* in 1659, and *Elena* in the 1660 season. Aureli similarly began producing librettos in a very leisurely way. His output in the 1650's included *Erginda* in 1652, *Erismena* in 1656, *Le Fortune di Rodope e di Damira* in 1657, *Medoro* in 1658 and *La Costanza di Rosmonda* in 1659. From 1657 to 1665, when he began to work elsewhere, he produced at least one libretto a year. 31 separate librettos of his were performed in Venice before 1709, which is the last known date in his life.

During the 1650's classical historical subjects began to be preferred for opera librettos, notably by Minato. *Xerse* and *Antioco* were followed in the next decade by *Scipione Affricano* (1664), *Muzio Scevola* (1665) and *Pompeo Magno* (1666). All five of these were set by Cavalli. Using a classical subject for a libretto, however, did not merely ential recounting the story. It had to be adapted for current Venetian tastes ('all' uso corrente', as Marco Faustini had put it), and moulded to fit the libretto pattern that continued to draw in the audiences. Not only historical endings but also entire motivations were changed, so that events of vast historical importance (for example the formation of the first Roman triumvirate between Pompey, Caesar and Crassus, which in *Pompeo Magno* II.2 is dismissed in a single page of recitative) were made completely subordinate to the amorous entanglements of the principals. The *argomenti* in Minato's librettos therefore consist of two sections. The first is entitled 'Di quello, che si hà dall'historia' and often even cites the classical source, for example Herodotus for *Xerse,* Plutarch for *Scipione Affricano*. This is immediately followed by 'Di quello che si finge', in which the characters and events, and the motivations behind them, are jumbled and reconstructed. For the purist there may be something improper in exploiting and distorting such a rich field of material. But Minato's candour about so doing is engagingly honest.

Aureli on the other hand preferred, like Faustini, to invent his own stories, and even turned back to mythology during the latter part of his career. Only occasionally did he follow Minato into history, with works like *Alessandro Magno in Sidone* (1679, set by M.A. Ziani) and *Pompeo Magno in Cilicia* (1681, set by Freschi), and also the two versions of *Eliogabalo* (1668, set first by Cavalli and then by Boretti), although here Aureli was revising the work of another poet. In the works of both Aureli and Minato, gods and goddesses disappeared almost completely, only appearing in Prologues. Aureli continued to add Prologues to most of his texts, but Minato soon tired of what were essentially irrelevant embellishments, and ceased to write them.

Concentration upon the aria gradually began to disrupt dramatic continuity in the 1660's and 1670's, but during the 1650's, in these early works of the new librettists, tight dramatic fluency was at its best. The thinning down of casts and the resulting greater intimacy of plots had removed most of the superfluous characters, and the librettists' aim was to tell a good story. Minato and Aureli were superb dramatists, both familiar with spoken drama, and their awareness of the necessity to keep up dramatic pace in opera produced a different type of recitative. A glance at any one of their librettos would illustrate this immediately. The standard eleven- or seven-syllable text layout is redistributed to give shorter, conversation-type lines. The syllables generally add up to the required number, but the dissection of the lines in this way results in recitative that is essentially quick-fire, fast-moving and therefore highly dramatic. Minato also used the stage aside, giving a further dimension of dramatic intensity, and even printed it 'a parte' in the libretto; and his texts are abundant with stage directions. His first libretto, *Orimonte*, serves as well as any to indicate the immediate changes that he initiated. The following dialogue occurs in the third act (scene 2):

CLEANTA:		Servi tua volontà
		Cosi hai prefisso, và
		Cor, e fè
		Mi sacrò.
ERNESTO	*(andante)*:	Ah crudel! ah mia vita!
CLEANTA	*(per se)*:	Ei per me,
		Lagrimò,
		E mal, s'io non l'arresto.
	(lo chiama)	Ernesto?
	(si pente)	Ah no son di Torindo.
ERNESTO	*(tornante)*:	Io corro a tuo comando.
CLEANTA	*(lo licentia)*:	Servi tua volontà.

Even faster moving and more entangled is the dialogue from *Xerse* (I.5) when all Adelanta's comments are made from her position 'sopra la loggia' and are therefore unheard by the others:

> ROMILDA: Speri ch'ei sia mio sposo? ADELANTA: Io spero. Ah temo.
> ARSAMENE: Si sarò. ROMILDA: Chirisponde?
> ARSAMENE: Son io Romilda amata. ADELANTA: Ah sconoscente?
> ROMILDA: Idolo mio? ARSAMENE: Sarò tuo sposo, si:

A dispetto ... ADELANTA: ... Di me. ROMILDA: Di chi? ARSAMENE: Del Rè.
ELVIRO: Presto, presto Arsamene.
Xerse viene. ARSAMENE: Empia sorte! ADELANTA: O bene a fè.
ROMILDA: Di chi temete? ARSAMENE: Lo saprete poi.
ELVIRO: Sù veloce fuggite.
ROMILDA: Sarà meglio celarvi. ADELANTA: Eh no, partite.
ELVIRO: Sù via l'ali a le piante.
ARSAMENE: M'ascondo. ROMILDA: State cauto. ARSAMENE: E voi costante.

Both Aureli and Minato were masters of dramatic situation. In Aureli's *Erismena* (II.4) there is a compelling sequence in which the disguised Erismena faints at the sight of her beloved. Erimante, who has ordered her to be killed, takes her for dead; and his intended wife Aldimira, deceived by Erismena's male disguise, revives her with an aria. In Minato's *Xerse,* just before the section quoted above, there are four characters, or sets of characters, on stage simultaneously, of whom all but one are unaware of the others' presence. These two superb theatrical moments were rarely equalled; possibly only in *Pompeo Magno* (1666), when at the end of the second act there is a splendid sequence of overhearing, mis-identification and murder in a darkened garden, did any librettist achieve such sophisticated theatricality. The use of this rapid-exchange dialogue inevitably meant the loss of poetry, but the need for it was perhaps diminished by the dramatic impetus gained from this new style of recitative. There were still moving aria texts, certainly, mostly at the inevitable laments, but the chief value of both these writers lay in their comic recitative. In addition to whole comic scenes there are countless examples in Minato of brief comic dialogue. In the second act of *Xerse* Elviro is disguised as a flower-seller, and four successive scenes are united by his refrain:

Ahi chi voler fiori
Di bella giardina?

In *Elena* (II.4) Ippolita and Eurite, both disguised as men, meet and nervously exchange the following witty dialogue:

IPPOLITA: Perche'l credi incostante?
EURITA: Perche lo veggio errante.
IPPOLITA: La costanza del cor non stà nel piede.
EURITA: Il peggior cieco è quel che tutto crede.

Such puns, epigrams and aphorisms aerate Minato's style enormously, giving it the pace and variety of a truly theatrical work.

After the intimacy of the 1650's, the tastes for larger effects, both aural and visual, brought about the return of larger casts. All three of Minato's mid-1660's historical librettos *(Scipione Affricano, Muzio Scevola* and *Pompeo Magno)* open with large crowd scenes. There are also increase in violence and realism. In *Scipione Affricano* a corpse is dressed up as one of the main characters and casually abandoned on stage; in *Muzio Scevola* the captured queen cuts off the head of the guard who has just raped her, and appears triumphantly with it (foreshadowing *Salome* by two and a half centuries); and in *Pompeo Magno* there is even a murder on stage. Such vivid realism was a far cry from the comparatively gentle and contemplative (and discreetly off-stage) fate of Daphne.

By this time, librettists were finding it increasingly difficult to satisfy the voracious appetites of their audiences. The demand for set-piece arias had constantly to be met, not only for the public, but also for the singers themselves. From about 1660 onwards, the librettists felt strongly enough about it to express their dissatisfaction and disillusionment in print. In 1665 Aureli wrote:

> The Venetian audiences have got to such a point that they no longer know how to enjoy what they see; nor do the authors know how to invent something to satisfy the bizarre tastes of this city. . . . Man cannot always work as he chooses, but he is constrained to obey the wishes of others.[27]

By 1673 he even went as far to admit, in the preface to *Claudio Cesare,* that he was continuing to produce librettos only for financial gain:

> As for me, suffice it to say that I write as much for he who pays, as for he who reads. I know that you understand me . . .[28]

At the end of the printed text there is a stop-press addendum, which includes yet three more arias; and this is accompanied by a note to the reader where Aureli now reveals his dejected attitude towards the singers. Not only, he says, must a writer take into account the capricious tastes of his audiences, but also the 'humori stravaganti de' Signori Musici recitanti'. Clearly, opera was now no longer the carefully integrated efforts of librettist and composer that it had been in the earlier days, and the gradual decline to the inflexible format of the eighteenth-century libretto was ineluctable. The dramatic peak of the 1650's was not to be reached for over a century.

NOTES

1. There is no comprehensive modern study of the seventeenth-century libretto, but for general considerations, see: A. Belloni: *Il Seicento* (Milan, 1929). H. Prunières: 'I libretti dell'opera veneziana nel seicento' in *RassM* III (1930), pp.441–448. F. Vatielli: 'Operisti-librettisti dei secoli XVII e XVIII' in *RMI* XLIII (1939), pp.315-332. U. Rolandi: *I libretti per musica attraverso i tempi* (Rome, 1951). P. Smith: *The Tenth Muse* (London, 1971).
2. For discussions of the *Camerata* and of early operatic ventures, see: N. Pirrotta: 'Temperaments and tendencies in the Florentine Camerata' in *MQ* XL (1954), pp.169–189. C. Palisca: 'The Alterati of Florence: pioneers in the theory of drama and music' in *New Looks at Italian Opera (Essays in Honor of D.J. Grout)* (ed. William Austin, Ithaca, 1968), pp.91ff. C. Palisca: 'The "Camerata fiorentina": a Reappraisal' in *Studi musicali* I (1972), pp.203–236.
3. *La Pellegrina:* (i) ed. H. Goldschmidt in *Studien zur geschichte der italienischen Oper im 17 Jahrhundert* (Leipzig, 1901–2) I, pp.374–380. (ii) ed. D.P. Walker in *Musique des intermèdes de 'La Pellegrina'* (Paris, 1963).
4. For a general discussion of the Daphne legend, see: Y. Giraud: *La fable de Daphné* (Geneva, 1969).
5. See N. Pirrotta: *Li due Orfei da Poliziano e Monteverdi* (Turin, 1969).
6. For opera in Rome, see: A. Ademollo: *I teatri di Roma nel secolo decimosettimo* (Rome, 1888). N. Pirrotta: 'Early Opera and Aria' in *New Looks at Italian Opera* (*op. cit.*), pp.39–107.
7. For Rospigliosi, see: C. Canevazzi: *Papa Clemente IX poeta* (Modena, 1900).
8. '. . . è lecito ai Poeti non solo alterare le Favole, mà le Istorie ancora' (in the preface to the printed libretto).
9. For Busenello, see: A. Livingston: *La vita veneziana nelle opere di Francesco Busenello* (Venice, 1913). A.A. Abert: 'Busenello' in *MGG* II

(1952), pp.511–513. T. Walker: 'Busenello' in *Grove* 6 (forthcoming).

10. It is not certain that *Giulio Cesare* was ever set, partly because no score survives, and partly because there is doubt about any operatic performance in the 1646 season. For discussions of this problem, see above, Chapter I, note 39.

11. In *Minerva al Tavolino* (Venice, 1681, 1688).

12. '. . . Se gli Atti sono cinque e non tre, rammentati, che tutti i Drammi antichi, e particolarmente le Trag. di Seneca son distruite in 5 Atti. Ne ti paia strano le mutazione de' luoghi, perche chi scrive non crede far peccato à modo suo. . . . riccordandoti sempre della lode che diede Tacito à Seneca, cioè che l'haveva un'ingegno fatto à posta per i giusti di quei tempi.'

13. pp.369–371, 385–389.

14. Hand A from the calligraphy chart in Chapter III. See below.

15. A flash of Busenello's humour appears in the *argomento* of *Statira:* 'Statira Donna e Giovane, e per consequenza indocile al tacere . . .'

16. For Faustini, see: A.A. Abert: 'Faustini' in *MGG* II (1954), pp.1881–1883.

17. '19 dicembre 1651. Il signor Zuane Faustini del quondam signor Anzolo d'anni 36 da mal maligno giorni 3'. (ASV, Necrologia 1651, f.877).

18. '. . . essendo stato troppo prematuramente rapito dalla morte l'anno 1651, nel trigesimo secondo dell' età sua . . .'

19. I am grateful to Professor Denis Arnold for pointing out that the same records miscalculated Monteverdi's age at his death.

20. 'Il Sogetto di questo Drama uscì dal Felicissimo ingegno del già Sign. Giovanni Faustini di famosa memoria; e della cui Virtù stupirono i Teatri non solo di questa Città, mà quelli ancora de' più remoti Paesi. Molte penne sublimi son state richieste, doppo la di lui Morte, à vestirlo col manto della Poesia, e con varie ragioni ciascuno à rifusato. Io non ò saputo rifiutar quest' honore, e benche mi frenasse la risolutione la mia debolezza, l'hà però stimolata il sapere, che se son stato compatito nel Xerse, nell' Artemisia, e nell' Antioco, ch'erano miei sogetti, ripieni delle mie debolezze, meglio sarò tolerato in questo, dove hò il fondamento del soggetto di Virtuoso tanto insigne. Prego il Cielo, che la Pace delle sue Ceneri non resti turbata da chi delle mie imperfettioni prenda ardimento di farne alla di lui Virtù qualche tocco. Mi dichiaro però che, ciò, che v'è di male è mio, e tutto ciò, che vi risplende di buono è suo. Tu Lettor Cortese ammirà il Sogetto,compatisci le Parole: e vivi felice.'

21. ASV, Scuola Grande di S Marco, b.188, f.82. Letter to Faustini.

22. 'Il Signor Giovanni Faustini nell'eta sua più giovenile per diletto proprio applicò l'ingegno alle compositioni Drammatiche Musicali, nelle quali riuscì ammirabile nell'inventione in particolare; Onde nel corso di soli anni nove (essendo stato troppo prematuramente rapito dalla morte

l'anno 1651, nel trigesimo secondo dell'età sua) si viddero rappresentare ne i Teatri di questa Città con gli applausi maggiori la Virtù de Strali d'Amore, l'Egisto, l'Ormindo, il Titone, la Doriclea, l'Ersilda, l'Euripo, l'Oristeo, la Rosinda, la Calisto, l'Eritrea, e doppo la di lui morte ancora l'Eupatra, poi l'Elena rapita da Teseo, vestita col manto di Poesia da sublime virtuoso, tutte poste in Musica, ò dalla virtù singolare del Signor Francesco Cavalli dignissimo Organista della Serenissima Republica, ò dal signor Pietro Andrea Zianni hora Maestro di Capella della Maestà dell'Imperatrice, incontrarono non solo nel genio, e nella sodisfattione di questa Citta tanto delicata nell'udire simili rappresentationi, mà di molte altre principali dell'Italia, nelle quali, più, e più volte sono state rappresentate con ogni pienezza d'applauso; anzi che con l'Inventioni multiplici, e varie d'esse quasi come di cose obliate si sono addobbate, e arrichite altre compositione.'

23. 'Il presente Drama fù lasciato imperfetto dal già Signor Giovanni Faustini, mentre ne compose solamente due Atti, mà d'ariette, e la maggior Parte in stille recitativo, come s'accostumava in quel tempo. Onde per ridurlo all'uso corrente è stato necessario che vi s'affatichi più d'una penna; senza alterar punto il Soggetto, e il scenario lasciato dall'Auttore in tutta perfettione, come anco il Prologo. . . . Per solo cappo di Brevità si tralasciano di recitare li versi contrasegnati con una vergola in margine. Onde potrai scorerli, che non levano punto l'intelligenza del Drama. Compatirai anco qualche errori di Stampa, che per la fretta è seguita.'

24. It is interesting that this move was similarly taking place in Rome. Rospigliosi's *Del male il bene* of 1653 has only six characters—two pairs of lovers and two servants—and this pattern was becoming very popular with the fast-developing *opera buffa.* In the following century it became the standard form for *opera seria*, and culminated in da Ponte's *Cosi fan tutte.*

25. For Aureli, see: E.A. Cicogna: *Illustri muranesi richiamati alla memoria* (Venice, 1858). C. Mutini: 'Aureli' in *Dizionario Biografico degli Italiani* IV (1972), pp.587–8. A.A. Abert: 'Aureli' in *MGG* I (1949–51), pp.859–862.

26. For Minato, see: E.C. Salzer: 'Teatro italiano in Vienna barocca' in *RID* I (1938), p.47ff. A.A. Abert: 'Minato' in *MGG* IX (1961), pp.348–350. E. Rosand: 'Minato' in *Grove* 6 (forthcoming).

27. Preface to *Perseo*, performed at the Teatro SS Giovanni e Paolo with music by Mattioli. 'Sò, ch'il gusto del Popolo di Venetia è arrivato à tal segno, che non sà più che bramar di vedere, nè i Compositori sanno più che inventare per sodisfar al capriccio bizarro di questa Città. . . . Non sempre l'Huomo opera per propria elettione, mà tal'hora è costretto ad affatticarsi per ubedire à chi può commandarli.'

28. Performed at the Teatro S Salvatore, music by Boretti. '. . . Quanto à me basta solo avisarti, ch'io compono più per chi spende, che per chi legge. Sò, che m'intendi. . . .'

CHAPTER III

The Operas

General survey

It is an ever-present temptation to the music-historian to slice a composer's output into convenient portions and then to label these as coming from specific 'periods' of the composer's style. Such a practice is inevitably unsound, for a composer does not often have violent changes of style during the course of his productive life (unless, perhaps, he is Stravinsky). Any development occurs partly through the process of the composer's own maturing and on the basis of his experience (and this progression is continuous up to a certain age, when usage hardens into habit), and partly through external influences, such as economics and public taste. Nevertheless, a composer can be seen to pass through various phases during the course of his career, and in a general consideration of Cavalli's operas a certain pattern may be observed.

In his first opera, *Le Nozze di Teti e di Peleo,* Cavalli was experimenting with the new art-form of combining music and drama, as indeed were all his Venetian contemporaries. This theatrical adolescence necessarily persisted for some years, and it was not until his partnership with Giovanni Faustini had produced several operas that any stability in his own operatic style, and in the form itself, began to be apparent. Between, perhaps, *Ormindo* (1644) and the last Cavalli-Faustini collaboration, *Eritrea* (1652) there was a general consolidating of operatic form and habit, and *Eritrea* itself may be said to represent a landmark in the composer's theatrical career. After Faustini's death, the younger generation of librettists injected a new vitality and a greater dramatic intensity into the medium, and Cavalli's operas from the 1650's reveal a near-perfect union of music and drama that he never achieved at any other time. By 1660 and his visit to France he was, as he admitted, becoming preoccupied with his age and his health, and his interest was anyway diversified into the commercial prosperity of his estate on the mainland. His unfortunate experiences in France seem almost to have quenched any theatrical passion remaining in him. When, in 1664, Marco Faustini persuaded him to renew his connection with him and his theatrical associates, Cavalli produced a trilogy of historical operas; but the spontaneity of the 1650's was now replaced by a rather set attitude to drama, whereby the musical highlights stood out from an almost mediocre background, rather than contributing to a coherent and consistent whole. By now, public taste had overtaken Cavalli and his own style was antiquated. His last operas either failed to reach the stage, or were performed outside the city in which operatic developments were first made. So the overall pattern of Cavalli's operas traces a curve, which is not particularly common. Monteverdi had had two distinct periods of operatic composition, at the Mantuan court and in the Venetian public theatres, separated by several years; but each was of outstanding merit and achievement. Mozart's 22 dramatic works generally followed an ever-ascending trend, with the result that his final operas marked the zenith of his entire dramatic *oeuvre.* (It is of course true that Mozart died at the height of his career.) But Cavalli's operas gradually rose to a peak in the 1650's and then declined from it; and for this reason we may perhaps be forgiven for regarding his operas in three groups, those of the ascent, those of the peak and those of the decline.

The specific characteristics of each period will emerge more clearly from a consideration of the individual ingredients of opera, such as aria and recitative. But some general observations can be made. Cavalli's early period, culminating with *Eritrea,* was one of general consolidation. The first operas relied heavily on prolonged sections of recitative, broken occasionally by strophic arias. Slowly the links between aria and recitative became more fluent and less perceptible, and Cavalli began to achieve the particular fluidity which became his hallmark. Special features which began to emerge were the lament in the middle of the third act, and the concluding love-duet, following the precedent of Monteverdi's *Poppea* of 1642.

The middle period, broadly the years of the 1650's was the perfection of the previous decade's endeavours. Cavalli's style was now fully fluent, with essentially through-composed arias growing out of their recitative background and dissolving back into it. There are remarkably few harsh divisions produced by perfect cadences and ritornellos to the extensive arias that were to dominate operatic style for the next century. The drama was never impeded by the music, nor the music by the drama. Each supported and enhanced, even embellished, the other in a manner rarely achieved after these years. Gradually the aria became more formalised, and towards the end of the decade there began to emerge longer, more obviously articulated, structures, foreshadowing the aria's domination of opera. It is not insignificant that the operas most frequently revived in the seventeenth century came from this central period: *Xerse, Erismena*, and also *Giasone* which, despite its slightly earlier date, must be included in this group because of the outstanding quality of Cicognini's text.

The final group of operas, from *Ercole Amante* onwards, shows the slow decline. Although there are some superlative individual arias and some compelling dramatic moments, operatic proprieties had clearly undergone change. The return of the chorus laid the emphasis on dramatic spectacle, and the lengthier, more elaborate, arias reflected the audience's predilection for individual singers. Recitative was more automatic and less intense. In comparison with his contemporaries Ziani, Castrovillari, Boretti, Cesti and Pallavicino, Cavalli's style was quite clearly lacking in novelty, and he gradually withdrew from theatrical prominence.

—— *Sources* ——

Cavalli's extant operas survive in the Contarini collection of the Biblioteca Marciana in Venice.[1] This remarkable source of manuscript music passed in the 1840's from the Contarini family to the Marciana. It contains, along with some chamber music and cantatas, a large number of opera scores which constitute the main body of surviving seventeenth-century Venetian opera. There are 113 complete scores of 108 operas, with four duplicates. Some scores are not completely identified, but the majority of them cover the period 1639 to 1684, and illustrate the work of 28 composers.

The history of this distinguished private collection, and how it became available to the public, is by no means fully clear. It was amassed by Marco Contarini, a member of the ancient and celebrated family which provided five Doges in the seventeenth century alone.[2] Marco was evidently more interested in the arts than in politics. During the 1670's he supervised the extension and redecoration of the magnificent villa at Piazzola, developments which included the building of a vast theatre accommodating 1000 people.[3] The theatre opened in November 1679 with a performance of Pallavicino's *Le Amazone nelle Isole Fortunate* (on a Piccioli libretto). The luscious and extravagant splendour which surrounded the whole occasion initiated a series of operatic events, in which the social significance predominated and the opera performance itself was merely one item in the programme of a day's entertainment. Nonetheless the whole promotion was based on Marco Contarini's genuine love of opera and his passionate desire that such works should be newly presented on his own premises.

It would seem that, shortly after the opening of the Teatro Contarini at Piazzola, he began to collect opera scores and to display them in his library. He acquired not only the works performed at Piazzola,[4] but also as many scores from Venice as he could find. The earliest score from the collection (Cavalli's *Le Nozze di Teti e di Peleo* of 1639) is only two years later than the beginning of public opera in Venice; and as the latest score dates from 1684 (Freschi's *Dario*) the collection as a whole fully reflects the development of Venetian opera in almost half a century of its existence. No further work was added to the collection after 1684, and as Marco Contarini died in 1689, it is reasonable to suppose that the whole venture was founded on his enthusiasm and ceased at his death.

Precisely how these scores were acquired remains puzzling, the more so because the majority date from before 1679. In particular the 28 scores of Cavalli present a problem. It is almost certain that Cavalli and Marco Contarini would have been acquaintances if not friends, and it is therefore possible to speculate that there might have been some agreement whereby Marco was to receive all Cavalli's opera scores for his library. But no such agreement is mentioned in his will, which in all other respects is meticulous in detail; and Marco Contarini did not begin collecting scores until 1681, by which time Cavalli had been dead for five years. The nature of the whole transaction is therefore completely in doubt. It does not even appear that the scores arrived at Piazzola in bulk, but that they were acquired singly and gradually. A printed volume of Frescobaldi keyboard toccatas,[5] which appears to have been part of the Contarini music collection and thus came to the Marciana during the last century, bears on its inside cover a fascinating list of operas. This list is written in a hand recognisable as that which identifies many of the Contarini opera scores by a title and sometimes even a composer's name at the top of the first page. The list reads as follows:

1681 originali di opere cantate

1. Il Ciro del Cavalli
2. L'Eritrea del Cavalli
3. Le Fortune di Rodope e di Damira del Ziani
4. L'Erismena del Cavalli
5. Le Fortune di Pirro del Ziani
6. Il Seleuco dell' Sartorio
7. Gl' Amori Infruttuosi di Pirro del Sartorio
8. I Duo Tiranni al Soglio del Sartorio Ant°
9. L'Ercole sul Termedonte Sartorio
10. Il Giulio Cesare del Sartorio
11. L'Antonino, e Pompregiano del detto
12. L'Anacreonte del detto
13. L'Eraclio Ziani
14. L'Enea in Italia Pallavicino

1682

15. Pompeo Magno Cavalli
16. L'Appollo del D. Gio. Batt. Rovetta
17. L'Erginda del D. Gaspare Sartorio
18. Il Marcello del Rovetti
19. Il Giasone Cavalli
20. Il Dario
21. L'Argia del Cesti
22. Claudio Cesare Boretti
23. Il Tito Boretti
24. Orfeo del S Ant° Sartorio
25. L'Adelaide Ant° Sartorio
26. Prosperita di Sejano Ant° Sartorio

27. Alcina di Ant° Sartorio, che non fu recitata
28. Antigona del Ziani

1683

29. Attila del Ziani
30. Diocletiano Pallavicino
31. Ratto del Sabine di Pier Simon Agustini

From this list it would appear that three separate batches of scores were received in 1681, 1682 and 1683. There are five scores by Cavalli among them: *Ciro* of 1654, *Eritrea* of 1652, *Erismena* of 1656, *Pompeo Magno* of 1666 and *Giasone* of 1649. *Pompeo Magno* was Cavalli's latest datable opera. The other four all had revivals in the 1660's and 1670's: *Ciro* was revived in 1665, *Eritrea* in 1661 and *Erismena* after 1670. *Giasone,* one of the most popular of all seventeenth-century operas, had 24 revivals in various parts of Italy and its score would have been in constant circulation. It would therefore seem likely that Cavalli's latest scores arrived at Piazzola first, and that the others followed at unknown intervals. Whatever process was involved in their transport from Venice to Piazzola, it was one of the most felicitous transactions for the history of opera; for at a time when no theatre music reached the security of the printing presses it preserved for posterity invaluable scores which would otherwise have sunk into oblivion, as did so many of their contemporaries.

In whatever manner the opera scores arrived at Piazzola, it appears that they were amassed quite quickly. In 1685 the Duke of Braunschweig and Lüneburg visited Piazzola, and the catalogue and timetable of events celebrating his visit was published at the villa's own printing press.[6] The eight sections which comprise this catalogue describe in some detail the state and appearance of Piazzola at the time, and one of them notes that there were many musical scores in the library: 'una gentil libreria copiosa di molti volumi. . . .'

For over 160 years after Marco Contarini's death, the music collection remained on the shelves of the 'gentil libreria'. In 1839 Girolamo Contarini, one of the last of the great family, wrote a will which was duly executed after his death in 1843;[7] in it he left the entire contents of his library to the Biblioteca Marciana in Venice. On 22 September 1843 the family solicitor Pietro Gardani approached the current librarian of the Marciana, Pietro Bembo. By 31 July 1844 all the legal ends were tied up. The whole collection, including 956 manuscripts and 4673 printed books became available to the general public.

Calligraphically, there are several hands in the collection's 113 scores. It seems that, on arrival at Piazzola, any untidy score was recopied by one of the several scribes in the Contarinis' employ, before being bound, gilded and shelved, But not all the scores were so improved, for most of Cavalli's seem to be in the state in which he left them. Seven are still in his autograph, while eight others also bear his markings. Their well-worn appearance, with much evidence of re-thinking, contrasts vividly with the neat state of the rest of the collection. Again it is paradoxically advantageous that the less than total efficiency of the Contarini library staff, who failed to treat all incoming manuscripts with equal care, has preserved autograph scores which reveal so much better than all others exactly how a composer worked.

Cavalli's 28 extant scores present several problems, for they show five regular hands, and two others. They are as follows:

1639	*Teti e Peleo*					D	
1640	*Apollo e Dafe*						X
1641	*Didone*	FC"				D"	X
1642	*La Virtù*					D	
1643	*Egisto*					D	
1644	*Ormindo*					D	
1645	*Doriclea*	FC"				D	
1649	*Giasone*					D	

1650	*Orimonte*	FC"		B			
1651	*Oristeo*	FC		B"			
	Rosinda	FC					
1652	*Calisto*	FC"		B			
	Eritrea					D	
1653	*Veremonda*	FC"			C		
	Orione	FC					
1655	*Xerse*	FC	A"				
1656	*Statira*	FC	A"				
	Erismena (I)					D	

1657	*Artemisia*	FC	A"			
1658	*Ipermestra*	FC	A"			
1660	*Elena*	FC"		C		
1662	*Ercole Amante*	FC"	A			
1664	*Scipione Affricano*				D	
1665	*Muzio Scevola*				D	
	Ciro (revival)					X
1666	*Pompeo Magno*				D	
1668	*Eliogabalo*	FC"			D	
?1671	*Erismena* (II)				D	

FC = Cavalli autograph
X = Miscellaneous
" = sections

The neat hand D, which has copied 13 complete scores, appears in no other score of the Contarini collection, suggesting that this particular scribe was employed by Cavalli himself. The scores written in Hand D give the chart a remarkable symmetrical pattern, for with the exception of *Eritrea* and the first *Erismena* score, they are all either earlier than 1650 or later than 1662, when Cavalli returned from France. I suggest as a working hypothesis that, towards the end of his life (probably around 1670), Cavalli employed a scribe to make fair copies of all his opera manuscripts. The scribe began with the most recent scores: that is, the five composed since his return, together with *Eritrea* (revived in 1661) and *Erismena* (revived after 1670). He then went back to the beginning of Cavalli's collection, and, leaving out *Apollo e Dafne* and *Didone,* worked steadily through in chronological order. His task was apparently never completed, for after *Giasone* the regularity ceases. Thus the scores from the 1650's, and also *Ercole Amante* of 1662, are in the hand either of the composer himself, or of people closely associated with him. It is probable that Hands A, B, and C were all Cavalli's pupils who worked with him on the preparation of scores. It is tempting to include among these Caliari, the favourite pupil to whom Cavalli left most of his music, and indeed to suggest that he was Hand A. Caliari was with Cavalli in Paris, and the score of *Ercole Amante* is mainly written in Hand A with Cavalli's additions. Certainly Hand A worked most closely with

Cavalli. In *Statira,* complete sections in Hand A appear between those in Cavalli's hand; and in *Artemisia* the whole of the third act is in Hand A. In both these scores, the sections in Cavalli's hand are in the familiar, untidy autograph state which suggests immediate and spontaneous composition, whereas those in Hand A are neat and fluent. It would seem that the pupil A was copying into the score sections which had already been composed by Cavalli, and which now had merely to be inserted into the main text.

Hand B copied out *Orimonte* and *Calisto* for Cavalli. It is also found in the Contarini score of Monteverdi's *L'Incoronazione di Poppea*, writing out the whole of Acts I and III, and most of the Prologue. Cavalli's hand is also in the score, and it is very likely that if there was a revival of *Poppea* in 1646[8] it would have been directed by Cavalli. His markings in the score are predominantly those of one who prepares a work for performance (for example 'un tuon più alto', and his possession of a score of this opera, written out by his own pupils, would account for its progress to the Contarini collection. The second score of *Egisto*, now in Vienna, is also in Hand B, supporting the suggestion that B was a pupil who made copies for his master, either for present or for future productions.

Veremonda and *Elena* are in the same hand, C. Like Hand D, this appears nowhere else in the Contarini collection, so it must again be assumed that this particular copyist was associated with Cavalli himself rather than with Piazzola. Again Cavalli's own hand appears in both scores, particularly in *Veremonda* where he has altered and extended the score quite considerably, as if reworking it for a revival. As with *Statira* and *Artemisia,* Cavalli has worked closely on these two operas with his scribe, who was probably therefore a pupil. (Given the fact that *Elena* was based on a Faustini libretto, it is even possible that this opera was composed earlier than its performance date of 1660 suggests. This would bring it closer to the composition of *Veremonda.*)

Cavalli's hand appears in three scores written out in Hand D, the copyist probably employed by him. In the *Doriclea* score[9] it can be found giving occasional corrections and directions[10] which suggest revision for a particular performance. In 1665 Marco Faustini wished to have his brother's libretto of *Doriclea* performed again, and Ziani rather reluctantly provided a new setting. It is therefore possible that Faustini temporarily considered reviving Cavalli's original setting. Similar autograph directions appear also in the

Muzio Scevola score.[12] As this opera was also revived outside Venice on several occasions, it is likely that Cavalli supervised a further copying of the score. The other score in which both Cavalli's hand and Hand D appear is *Didone,* but here the main bulk of the copying has been done by a strange hand, found in no other score of the Contarini collection. Since *Didone* was revived at least twice, in Naples (1650) and Genoa (1652), it is possible that this copyist was preparing a new score from Cavalli's original manuscript.[12] He evidently had some difficulty in deciphering Cavalli's handwriting, for he had to leave many gaps, the most crucial of which (for example the string parts in III.3) were supplied by Cavalli himself. There are also further directions in Cavalli's hand (such as 'Tutti qui entrano, col'raddopio di Voci et Instromenti', f.99) which again suggest that this score was destined for a non-Venetian company. Hand D has also gone through the *Didone* score, as if tidying up the difficult passages left by both Cavalli and the foreign scribe.

As the list of titles in the volume of Frescobaldi toccatas shows, *Ciro* was one of the first operas to arrive at Piazzola, and it has been recopied by a scribe in whose hand are no fewer than 32 operas and a volume of cantatas. The score does not correspond either to the 1654 or the 1655 libretto, and it is therefore probably a replica of the 1665 revival. The *Apollo e Dafne* score survives in another hand which is totally alien both to Cavalli's operatic *corpus* and to the rest of the Contarini collection. It almost seems that this score arrived at Piazzola through a different source from its fellows, and the fact that the opera was revived in Bologna in 1647 provides a possible solution to this final calligraphical puzzle.

—— *Method of composition* ——

The 22 copies or partial copies of Cavalli's scores show many very obvious scribal errors, such as wrong clefs or accidentals, or faulty underlay. But since these copies seem to have been made at his suggestion, and often with his supervision and participation, they can be assumed to be relatively accurate. Ritornellos without upper string parts, for example, have often been left in that state, with no attempt made at realisation. All 28 of Cavalli's scores can therefore be considered as a whole for stylistic observations. As definitive archetypes there are the precious autographs, which show very clearly just how the composer worked. Cavalli's music is always inspired by the text or by the situation. He seems to have worked straight through the libretto from beginning to end, writing rapidly and fluently according to the requirements of the text. He then went back and altered various passages, filling in string parts and perhaps rewriting complete sections; but the spontaneity and immediacy of his initial reaction to the libretto still survive the various layers of correction and alteration.

It is this spontaneity that supplies the scores with certain incongruities. There are four occasions where a character changes clef and therefore range within the course of the opera, and several others where a character briefly slips into another clef. In *Oristeo* (II.13) the part of Oristeo himself, hitherto a baritone, is suddenly written in the bass clef. In the first act of *Rosinda* the part of Rudione alternates disconcertingly between alto and bass clefs. In *Eritrea* (II.13) the alto Theramene becomes a baritone. And in *Scipione Affricano* (III.14) Siface's part goes from the alto clef to the bass clef. These changes are the most difficult phenomenon in Cavalli's scores. In the latter two cases, it would seem that Cavalli wrote the parts lower in range in order to spread out the voices in the final quartet, although this now raises the question of whether the same singer could and would sing both alto and baritone. The *Oristeo* instance could have been a lapse in concentration, but the range and tessitura in which the unfortunate singer must spend the rest of the opera are much lower than those of the first half. The *Rosinda* problem is the most complex. It seems that Cavalli had in mind a particular singer (an alto) when he began to write the opera, and learned that this singer had been replaced by a bass only after the completion of the first four scenes. From Act I scene 5 onwards, Rudione was therefore written in the bass clef. Cavalli thought it necessary to rewrite Rudione's earlier solo scene for the new singer, though the less important interjections of recitative in the remaining scenes could be worked out in rehearsal.

Cavalli's spontaneous reaction to the text brings out further surprising details in composition. As has already been shown, the librettist supplied the composer with a clear idea of which text was for an aria, and which for recitative, depending on the number of syllables in a line. On many occasions Cavalli completely ignored such guidance, and set the text as he thought fit. This was a habit from his earliest opera onwards. In *Le Nozze di Teti e di Peleo* (III.5) the scene is textually laid out as recitative and a three-stanza aria for Peleo. Cavalli chose to set the entire text as recitative. Apart from a short bass pedal of two bars at the beginning of each stanza of text, there is no connexion between them. Similarly in *Egisto*, four years later, the long mad scene for Egisto himself (III.5) was completely restructured by Cavalli. Faustini apparently intended it to begin with a two-stanza aria with a common refrain, aria being heavily implied by the use of six-syllable and five-syllable lines:

Celesti fulmini,
Onde vastissime,
Cupe voragini,
Leone Getuli,
Abbrusciatela,
Sommergetela,
Inghiottitela,
Divoretela.
(etc.)

But Cavalli sets the whole scene (over four pages of libretto and nine of score) as recitative, using devices such as pedal points, wide leaps and strange dissonances, occasionally moving into arioso or small $\frac{3}{2}$ sections for very short periods. This apparently inconsequential structure emphasises the prevalent insanity of the character, and makes this scene one of the most powerful and remarkable that Cavalli ever wrote. There are countless other instances where Cavalli has turned down the offer of an aria, presumably knowing that the aria would threaten the dramatic fluency of the scene. In *Eritrea* (II.12) he even refuses a duet. The text is set out as follows, with lines of equal length and rhyming between them:

LAODICEA: Raggio de gl'occhi miei
ERITREA: Morta, che sia costei.
LAODICEA: Adorata sembianza
ERITREA: Lieta rinvedira la mia speranza.
(etc.)

The urgent situation of this scene, however (a messenger has just announced that the city is being besieged and that Eritrea must flee) evokes its own reaction from Cavalli, who sets the duet as recitative.

Conversely Cavalli could pull arias out of recitative text. In *Statira* (III.5), Busenello laid out the whole scene between Floralba and Vaffrino as recitative. But at Floralba's 'Io vivo nè sò più à chi' the metre becomes $\frac{3}{2}$, simply growing out of the recitative text. There are very many instances in Cavalli's music where small, perhaps ten-bar, sections of triple time emerge from, and dissolve back into, the main recitative background; but on this occasion what appears is a much more prolonged piece (of 33 bars) with a recognisable shape. The opening of the $\frac{3}{2}$ section suggests that this is to be yet another ground-bass aria (there are four in this opera), with a descending A major scale as its bass formula. There are in fact only two intact statements of this scale; the third alters halfway through, and thereafter there is no binding shape. But occasional scale motifs continue to appear in the bass line, showing that this aria is no mere momentary digression from the recitative text. Its inclusion also contributes greatly to the dramatic structure of the scene, for it is immediately followed by Vaffrino's statement: 'Sento d'armi rumor'. The impact of this moment is all the more startling when contrasted with the relaxed music immediately before it, and it is conceivable that Cavalli chose thus to treat the recitative text in order to create precisely this effect.

Cavalli could also mould a completely new shape on to a given structured text. In *Egisto* (I.4), Hipparco's solo scene opens with the aria 'Hor che del Ciel'. The text for this aria is set out in the libretto as eight lines of seven-syllable text framed by two lines of eleven-syllable text:

> Hor che del Ciel ne le stellate piaggie
> Sù l'indomite terga
> Del Toro il Sol s'asside;
> Hor che vezzeggia, e ride
> La gioventù de l'anno
> Di smeraldi adornata,
> La Cittade abbandono,
> E qui drizzo le piante
> Costante si, mà non gradito amante.

Cavalli takes the first three lines for an eight-bar phrase (of four plus four). The next four lines use the same music, with written-in ornamentation, but cadence once imperfectly with 'Di smeraldi adornata', and repeat the phrase with a perfect cadence to accommodate the next line. The remaining two seven-syllable lines repeat the ornamented version, breaking off after six bars to go into a six-bar syncopated phrase for the last line, which is itself repeated. By reshaping the text in this way, Cavalli has underlined the meaning of it, separating the various thoughts and building up to an appropriate setting of the last line.

The opening to the third act of *Elena* also shows how the length of the phrase was determined not so much by the textual phrase itself but by Cavalli's interpretation of it and his desire to adhere to its meaning. Here Menelao's aria 'Sospiri di foco', written in six-syllable lines, falls naturally into four-bar phrases:

> Sospiri di foco
> Che l'aure infiammate
> Leggieri volate
> Intorno al mio bene,
> E l'aspre mie pene
> Narrateli un poco;
> Sospiri di foco.

But Cavalli has written melismas on the words 'leggieri volate', thus extending the phrase to the unusual length of eleven bars:

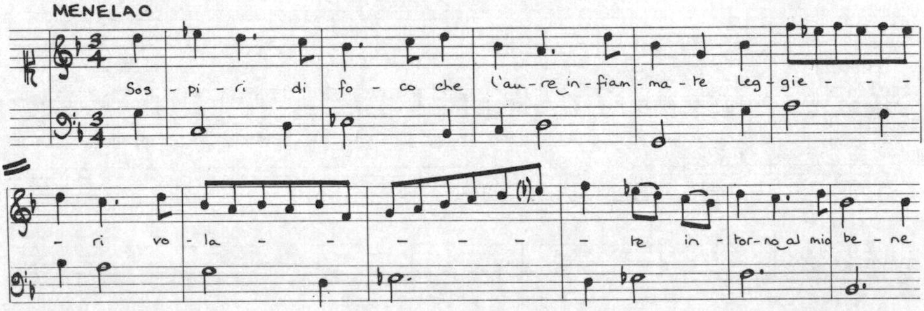

In the many librettos set by Cavalli, most of them moulded on much the same formula, there was obviously some duplication of situation and text. There are therefore instances where Cavalli reacts identically to similar situations or phrases in different librettos. In *Ormindo* (III.3) there is a prison scene in which two characters share a lament built over a ground bass with a sustained pedal in the accompanying violins. Eleven years later the prison scene in *Erismena* (III.15) was on such similar lines that Cavalli simply transferred the *Ormindo* music into the new opera, adapting the text as necessary.[13] On a smaller scale there are examples of particular phrases being set to the same music. In *Calisto* (II.10) Endimione's 'Cor mio, che vuoi tù?' bears a striking resemblance to Artemisia's passage in *Artemisia* (III.9), 'Cor mio, che sarà?':

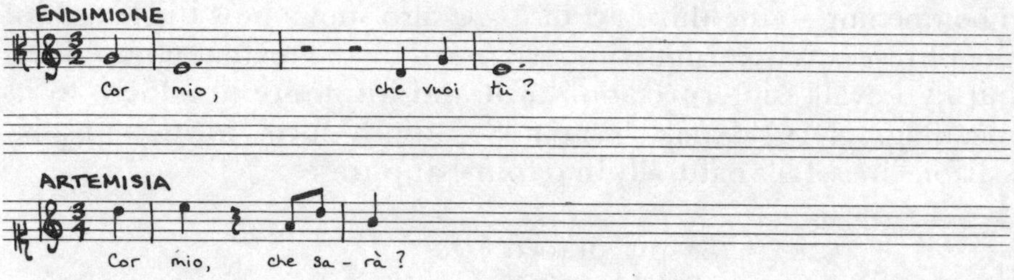

Similar musical phrases also occur where there is no apparent verbal connection, or even a link between sentiments. Diana's 'Vivi à nostri amori' from *Calisto* (II.2) is conspicuously similar both to Eumene's 'Di donar i serti' from *Xerse* (III.7) and to the Chorus 'Con la zampa, Eto e Piroo' from *Scipione Affricano* (I.2):

Both these types of musical duplication (some examples which are connected by text and others which are not) paradoxically illustrate the same point: that Cavalli's reaction to a libretto was fresh and spontaneous. The similar musical phrases which are based on similar textual phrases show that Cavalli's interpretation of a situation or mood was fairly consistent. Those which have no textual connection show that, rather like Handel, he wrote in a homogeneous style which was readily applicable in many and various situations.

Cavalli generally used the C sign to indicate quadruple time, and $\frac{3}{2}$ for triple time. After about 1655 there was a gradual move towards a preference for $\frac{3}{4}$, but this did not necessarily imply a faster tempo than $\frac{3}{2}$ unless the two were juxtaposed. There are also occasional uses of $\frac{6}{8}$ metre, and in *Le Nozze di Teti e di Peleo* (I.1) the celebrated *Chiamatta alla caccia* is noted in $\frac{12}{8}$. Key signatures are most often either bare or with one flat, adding accidentals as necessary. Very occasionally he uses a more advanced key signature, such as three sharps (for example in *Artemisia* I.12). The vocal parts are in the usual soprano, alto, tenor, baritone and bass clefs, with the very occasional use of a mezzo-soprano clef, and a single appearance of a treble clef (Amore in *Apollo e Dafne* II.3). The string parts, on the other hand, are almost always written in treble clefs. When soprano clefs appear in violin parts, this does not necessarily imply different instruments, but merely that the range of a particular piece has been lowered for dramatic purposes. In many cases, the change of register afforded by this juxtaposition of treble and soprano clefs in the string parts is startlingly effective. The Prologue to *Egisto* is sung by Notte ('che tramonta') and Aurora ('che sorge'). For Notte's music the violins are unusually written in soprano clefs, which change to treble clefs when Aurora appears. Similarly in *Rosinda* (I.6) the descent to the Underworld and the first appearance of Pluto are marked by the descent also into soprano clefs for the violins. At Proserpina's frivolous, teasing reply to Pluto's ardent protestations of love, the violins return to the treble clefs, and carry up the tessitura by more than an octave.

As the minimal key signatures imply, these scores date from what must (with reserve) be called the pre-tonal period. Thus there is not always a clear sense of home key, nor a strength of direction and organisation of keys. Frequently Cavalli finds it necessary to digress into a single-flat key-signature for a short period, and then abandon it, depending on the mood of the text. Full arias and other closed forms are firmly based on one tonal centre, to the extent that they begin and end in it; but the intermediary progressions are not always to closely related keys, nor are the cadences always on the closest degrees. There is thus a somewhat undisciplined overall effect. On top of this insecurity, chromaticism is heavily applied, particularly in laments or passages of affective recitative. It is noticeable that strong chromaticism is totally effective in areas with a firm idea of the home key, but is merely distracting and puzzling in those without one. Such apparently random choice of keys and progressions frequently lends considerable instability to Cavalli's music. This can only be overcome in performance by working from the immediate sense of the text, as

Cavalli did constantly, rather than by attempting to apply to a passage an overall harmonic shape which does not necessarily exist.

Rhythmically Cavalli's style also stems from the text, with arias and recitative both following speech inflections for the most part. Melismas on important and decorative words extend the rhythms and phrasing. In triple time Cavalli frequently uses hemiolas at cadences, in common with all other seventeenth-century composers; and he also dabbles in cross-rhythms elsewhere in the musical text. Not only does he stress phrases across the bar-line, but he also combines these with a *basso continuo* stressed differently across the bar-line, as for example during the melisma on 'cesserà' in Valeria's aria 'La fiamma ch'Amore nel core m'accese' (*Muzio Scevola,* I.16):

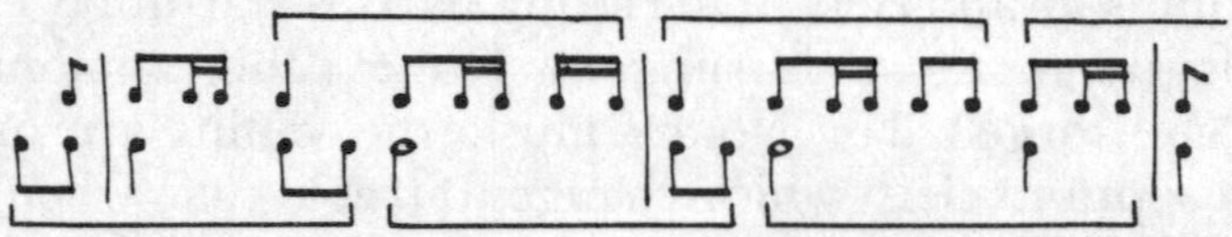

As with unsteady tonality, such insecurity in rhythmic stress and therefore direction only serves to confuse the listener, and the writing almost appears distracted. But there are occasions when Cavalli seems intentionally to have caused such confusion. Two of these occur in *Calisto.* The first is in the aria for Mercurio 'Se non giovano' (I.6). Its refrain 'Ch'ingannatore amante è quel che gode', is written in $\frac{3}{2}$, but the word-setting is such that a time signature of $\frac{4}{2}$ is distinctly implied:

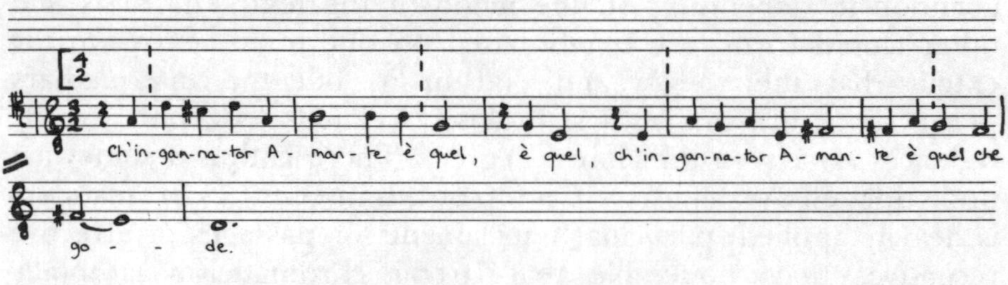

Secondly the Sattirino aria 'Chi crede à femina' (II.4) is also in $\frac{3}{2}$ with a crotchet rhythm. Here it is not the time signature or the metre which are in question, but the actual barring and consequently the word emphasis. Cavalli sets the text with the following rhythms:

Chi cre-de à fe-mi-na ne l'ac-que se-mi-na

whereas in performance it is difficult to point it in any other way than:

Chi cre-de à fe-mi-na ne l'ac-que se-mi-na

It is possible that Cavalli was deliberately barring these arias awkwardly in order to illustrate the prevalent mood of 'inganna-tore'. ('O what a tangled web we weave/When first we practise to deceive!')

Finally, in Eritrea (III.6), Lesbo's comic and rather naughty aria 'Sempre il gusto' is a fascinating example of rhythmic complexity. After the first phrase, built on eight textual stresses, Cavalli increases all subsequent phrases to nine stresses by using repetition or melisma. This means that the four phrases of the aria begin and end at different places in the bar. The general effect is to tease the audience musically as well as textually:

LESBO
Sem-pre il gus-to, e l'ap-pe-ti-to, pron-to, pron-to ha-ve-te. Ne vi sa-tia un sol ma-
-ri-to è in-dis-cre-te, in-dis-cre-te. Sem-pre il va-go, e sen-za af-fet-to, senz' a-mar vor-
-res-ti in let-to. Sem-pre il va-go, e sen-za af-fet-to, senz' a-mar vor-res-ti in let-to.

Despite Cavalli's close associations with St Mark's and his familiarity. with its polyphonic practices, he makes remarkably little use of counterpoint. Apart from a single case in *Ercole Amante* (III.1), where a duet does show distinct echoes of Gabrieli brass music:

there are few parallels to the traditions of contrapuntal church music, which, as Cavalli's own output shows, were still holding their own against the new style of monodic composition. But there are some semblances of counterpoint. Imitation between the voice and instruments occurs frequently, often at close intervals, and many ritornellos feature it strongly. In many arias in 4/4 time, the bass often moves constantly in crotchets or quavers throughout, even imitating parts from the vocal line, and thus producing almost a two-part invention, for example in *Muzio Scevola* (I.10):

But there is never prolonged counterpoint; for it is the nature of opera to concentrate on the solo voice, and not to confuse its ascendancy by the addition of quasi-equal parts.

— *Aria and closed form* —

The emergence of the aria[14] as a defined musical form was a gradual process. In the first operas of the Florentine and Mantuan composers, there were remarkably few completely closed forms, since it was the aim of composers and librettists to pursue the drama through the declamation of the text, or *stile recitativo.* Such set-piece arias as were composed served a specific dramatic purpose; in Monteverdi's *Orfeo* of 1607, for example, Orfeo's celebrated strophic aria 'Vi ricorda o boschi ombrosi' is sung in reply to a request from his fellow-shepherds:

Dunque fa degno ORFEO
Del suon della tua lira
Questi campi ove spira
Aura d'odor Sabeo.

Gradually the occasions where the dramatic action was halted temporarily for a period of contemplation or reflection became more frequent, and arias became an equal participant in the general musico-dramatic scheme. Eventually individual singers became so popular that they had to be given repeated opportunities to exhibit their voices and techniques to their adoring public; and the number of arias in an opera was therefore totally disproportionate to the number of dramatically suitable occasions for them. This gradual process towards the destruction of dramatic continuity by the over-dominance of individual arias began during the first thirty years of public opera in Venice. Since Cavalli's scores are almost the sole representatives of this period, they serve as a measure of the general evolution of the aria.

The earliest form, traceable back to the Florentine operas, was the stophic one. This had always been a form allowing for a certain amount of vocal display as strophes could be increasingly ornamented; this served the dual purpose of displaying the singer's technique and of intensifying the drama. ('Possente spirito' in the third act of Monteverdi's *Orfeo* was among the most striking early examples of this technique[15].) Very often in Cavalli's early operas his reaction to a strophed text was to set it as strophic variation, illustrating once again that his music was always text-inspired. The aria 'Musica, dolce musica' from *Apollo e Dafne* (I.4) is one of the many examples of this type of composition. Basically the vocal line in the two strophes is declamatory recitative in its adherence to speech rhythms. But illustrative melismas occur on individual words; each stanza is punctuated by a concluding ritornello; and in particular the bass line is identical in both strophes. This technique is one of measuring recitative; and as an effective method it was employed by Cavalli throughout his operas. There are therefore countless examples where, moved by the text, he goes into triple time for perhaps eight bars or less, or moves the bass into a steadily pulsating rhythm.

By the late 1640's and early 1650's, closed forms were becoming detached and various recognisable structures began to be in evidence. The first of these was the tripartite form ABA. Textually it had become common to emphasise the first line of a stanza by repeating it at the end. Gradually this practice increased so that the common lines at either end became more numerous, and in later years this developed into the full *da capo* form. The second form which arose during the late 1640's, ABB, had its origins in the technique of repeating the last line of a stanza to give it greater emphasis. Again the number of lines gradually increased so that as much as half the text could be repeated. Both ABA and ABB served a particular dramatic purpose: by repeating either the original part or the last section of the text, the overall message was underlined. But the basic difference was that the ABA structure was indicated in the libretto and was therefore a dramatic interpretation by the poet; whereas ABB form was applied according to the dramatic interpretation of the composer.

Although these two forms greatly increased in popularity during the 1650's, at the beginning of the decade they were very much subordinated to the through-composed aria. This category was generally reserved for serious characters, for its formlessness permitted of internal psychological development, and it was possible for a character to express a changing emotion within an aria. It is very likely that this technique was an extension of affective recitative, and that the measured, regular bass line was simply a means of defining the emotional contours of the text. A supreme example is Nerea's 'Oh mio dolce' from *Rosinda* (II.10). The irregularly-metred text gives Cavalli no lead for an aria:

Che mi vuoi morta? ohime rallenta Amore,
Non più rallenta l'arco,
Hò di strali novelli il petto carco.
Oh mio dolce spietato, oh mio fuggace,
Non sò come raccorti,
O nemico, ed amante. A la mia pace
Ogn'hor tù guerra apporti,
Incessante flagello
Sempre, sempre ti provo, ò caro, ò bello.
Per baciar la sua pena
L'alma da suoi recessi al labro è giunta,
Ma importuna honestà le sgrida, e affrena.

Yet he has chosen to illuminate Nerea's changing mental attitude by setting it over a measured bass, and therefore by putting it on to a slightly higher plane. Nerea is thinking aloud: her uncertainty as to how Clitofonte will react to her is communicated at the beginning of the aria, and by the end of it ('ma importune honestà le sgrida, e affrena') she has resolved to behave with dignity.

Among these through-composed arias, some have different sections in different time signatures, and this initially implies some sort of sectional formality. It seems, however, that the difference between $\frac{3}{2}$ and $\frac{4}{4}$ time was suggested to Cavalli entirely by the mood of the text and the interpretation of particular words or phrases, rather than by any desire to give purely musical variety; but this was of course a feature of Cavalli's composition as much in his formal as in his informal arias.

To all these three aria categories, formal or informal, the strophic technique could still be applied, and in some of these a fuller formal element was contributed by a specific textual refrain between stanzas. Strophic arias were generally sung by secondary characters (comic or immortal), for they were not part of the main story and it did not therefore matter if the action was temporarily halted because of a block of musical repetition. For the strophic condition is dramatically limiting: it can only portray a single emotion, and the simple, lighthearted feelings (such as lust, greed or fear) of the comic characters are best suited to this medium. Serious characters were occasionally also given strophic arias, but (in the 1650's) in one of only three sets of circumstances: either in a solo scene, where the dramatic pace has anyway slowed down to let an individual reflect upon his current situation; or in a sequence where two characters share a particular sentiment and therefore the strophes of an aria; or very occasionally where it is still dramatically feasible for a character to repeat his entire sentiment within the same music. In each case, the strophic form served a specific dramatic purpose, and so provided the contrast which is the essence of drama.

A very popular aria type, recurring through all Cavalli's operas, was the lament. This was often the musical highlight of the whole work, with the most organised formal structure, and the most sensuous vocal line. One of the principal serious characters, usually but not necessarily detached from the rest of the cast into a solo scene, laments his or her present predicament—be it unrequited love, solitude or imprisonment. The arias are usually in triple time; often with string accompaniement; and frequently over a ground bass. Both dramatically and musically these occasions were vitally important, and it was desirable to have at least one in each opera. A lament text was therefore fed to the composer by the librettist. It is interesting that in his early operas Cavalli had not yet evolved his formula for treating such texts. In *Teti e Peleo* the only lament (III.5) is set as recitative, as is the first of two in *Apollo e Dafne* (I.7). Busenello's poetry again excels, and is neatly structured by the use of a refrain 'Lassa, io m'inganno, io non son quella più'. Cavalli's music, with diminished intervals and pathetic cadences, responds ideally to the contrasts of the poetry, and makes the whole section one of his finest pieces of recitative. There is no doubt that it was considered by Cavalli as a lament, for in the score the passage is marked 'lamento'. Later in the same opera, however, there is another lament text, 'Misero Apollo' (III.3), which is partly set over a descending tetrachord bass pattern. With *Didone* in the following year he continued to set laments in a much more controlled and measured form. In the first act Cassandra and Ecuba sing laments, Cassandra for her dead betrothed Corebo, and Ecuba for the fall of Troy. Both are exquisitely set over ground bass patterns. Cassandra's strophic lament 'L'alma fiacca svanì' embodies a complete descending chromatic scale in D minor, while Ecuba's 'Tremula spirito' six-bar formula is also based on chromaticism. Other ground bass patterns followed, most of them based on some form of the minor descending tetrachord. (Cavalli was doubtless familiar with Monteverdi's 'Lamento della ninfa'[16].) These ground bass laments became so popular that in the mid-1650's several were included in each opera. *Erismena* has three; *Statira* has four. Laments did not always involve ground bass patterns; an irregular bass line was also used occasionally, but the aria was still generally in triple time and continued to make much use of suspension and dissonance between the voice and bass line, and the string parts if they existed. Cavalli frequently added string parts to his laments: not merely between the vocal entries within the aria, as was his standard practice, but continuously throughout the aria. One particular lament, from his last opera, illustrates the form at its most sophisticated and most moving. Alessandro's 'Misero' from *Eliogabalo* (I.13) has two strophes set over a ground bass and employs strings throughout. The lament was perhaps most successful when written over a ground bass. A relentless binding ostinato conveys much more poignantly the restraint of deep emotion.

co - si và che fe - del t'a - do - rò ?
Tra - di - tri - ce bel - tà, in - fe - li - ce, che fà ?
Stol - to, non m'a - vi - sa - i che con bel - tà fè non si tro - va ma - i.
Stol - to, stol - to non m'a - vi - sa - i che con bel -

-tà fè non si tro - va, non si tro - - - - va — ma - - i.

Cavalli could also employ a ground bass aria for dramatic purposes. In *Calisto* and *Eritrea,* Endimione's 'Vivo per te' (III.7) and Theramene's 'Volto amato' (I.8) are both set over a four-bar ground-bass pattern. Endimione and Theramene are both in some way detached from the rest of the cast, and not only by the miseries of unrequited love (for these are common feelings), although these miseries do partially account for the characters' introspection. But Endimione is the only mortal in *Calisto,* and he loves the immortal Diana, and Theramene is temporarily insane with grief at the supposed death of his lover. The arias for both characters underline their isolation and agitated mental states by making them unable to sustain such a controlled bass pattern. In each case the ground bass formula is interrupted, and the singer moves into recitative or less stable musical material.

In many cases, a strophic aria could be shared between two characters who sing alternate stanzas, and such pieces can be considered as horizontal duets. True duets occur most regularly in the final acts of operas, when the resolutions of the plot provide more opportunities for characters to sing together, and particularly at their conclusions. In the early operatic ventures of Florence and Rome, and in the subsequent French field, operas ended with huge tableaux involving the entire cast, chorus, ballet and even audience. Like the Prologue they often made reference to the dedicatee of the work, or the person in whose honour it was being performed, a tendency which in later France grew to grossly sycophantic levels. In Venice, however, where the occasion and therefore the audience were entirely different, operas did not require such endings. Audiences went to the opera to be entertained by a story enacted before them, and the opera finished when the story finished. It is here that the curious paradox of Venetian opera is apparent. For although it was essentially spectacular and glittering and of immediate impressive impact, the basis of the plot and its conclusion and outcome were intimate, even simple, with a traditional happy ending of resolved amorous entanglements. The most usual ending was therefore the love duet, or its own extension into a quartet or sextet depending on the number of pairs of lovers involved. (*Doriclea, Oristeo* and *Eritrea* end with quartets *Artemisia* with a sextet.) No fewer than 18 of Cavalli's 27 extant operas have a love duet or its extension in the last scene. Within these the form is somewhat varied. That at the end of *Didone* is preceded by a two-stanza aria of which Didone and Iarba each sing one strophe; the subsequent duet is built upon the same bass as the aria, but the vocal parts and instrumental lines differ. *Doriclea* is similar: two pairs of lovers each sing a duet of the same music with a ritornello, and join for the final quartet. A comparable scheme is found in *Eritrea.*

An alternative method of ending operas was with a lighthearted aria, generally sung by a secondary character, and perhaps with a slightly moralistic tone. (*Pompeo Magno,* for example, ends with Farnace's 'Imparate, ò mortali'.) Because this ending was not sung by any of the reunited lovers, it was possible to present the two methods consecutively. In *Artemisia,* for example, the sextet is followed by an aria from Eurillo, the court page-musician. If an opera ended in neither way then it would be swiftly and effectively brought to a close by a short ensemble, involving the people who happened to be around on stage. These ensembles are generally very short indeed, perhaps as little as four bars, so that the change of texture indicated that the opera was concluded. Just as the quartet and sextet were vertical extensions of the duet, so may these final ensembles be of moral aria conclusion.

Exceptions to these basic methods were the operas written for courtly events: *Orione* (for Milan), *Ipermestra* (for Florence), *Ercole Amante* (for Paris). All these are conscious of the occasion at their conclusion. *Orione* does in fact end with a sextet which in musical content is not dissimilar to those in *Veremonda* and *Artemisia*; but its text refers openly to the young Hapsburg, Ferdinand IV, in whose honour the opera was performed. It is interesting that although *Ipermestra* ends with a long epilogue involving the characters from the Prologue, the actual dramatic plot ends with love duets in the true Venetian fashion.

Duets where two characters sing on the same theme naturally occur at places before the end. There are also other, more pleasing, uses of the duet. In *Eritrea* (II.10) Laodicea's 'Speranza non giova' over a quasi-ostinato bass is taken up by Eritrea, whose 'Patienza mia face' uses the same music. In this piece the two characters do not sing together, but alternate within a single musical structure which binds the scene in a very satisfactory way. In *Elena* a whole scene (II.1) is unified by a bass in triple time, over which two couples converse with each other. Theseo and Peritoo open the conversation, which shortly passes to Creonte and Menesteo. Throughout the scene the two couples converse alternately, and finally sing together in the last line. Since Minato's text suggests no more than normal recitative, it is Cavalli's own intention to unite the scene in this way.

A further impressive duet technique of Cavalli's was using it to express the opposite emotions of two characters. The theme was most often still one of love. In *Oristeo* (I.7) Corinta and Oristeo sing at the same time, but about their separate attitudes to love. He, the optimist, is urging them to pursue their loves, while she advocates the reverse. Within the confines of a duet, Cavalli has differentiated between their two attitudes by means of long notes and dissonance for Corinta, and a more lively and ornamented vocal line for Oristeo:

Pe-na-re - te
fi-ne fes-to - - - si. Go-de-re - - -
Fug-gi-te-lo, fug-gi-te-lo, fug-gi-te-lo, fug-gi-te-lo. Go-dè, go-
-te. Se-gui-te-lo, se-gui-te-lo, se-gui-te-lo, se-gui-te-lo.
-dè chi lo sprez-zò.
Fug-gi-te-lo, fug-gi-te-
Go-dè, go-dè chi lo sdeg-ni. Se-gui-te-lo, se-
-lo, fug-gi-te-lo. No, no, no. Pe-na-re-te
-gui-te-lo, se-gui-te-lo. Si, si, si, si.
Fug-gi-te-lo, fug-gi-te-lo, fug-gi-te-lo, fug-gi-te-
Go-de-re - - - te. Se-gui-te-lo, se-gui-te-lo, se-gui-te-lo, se-
-lo. Go-dè, go-dè chi lo sprez-zò.
-gui-te-lo. Go-dè, go-dè chi lo sdeg-

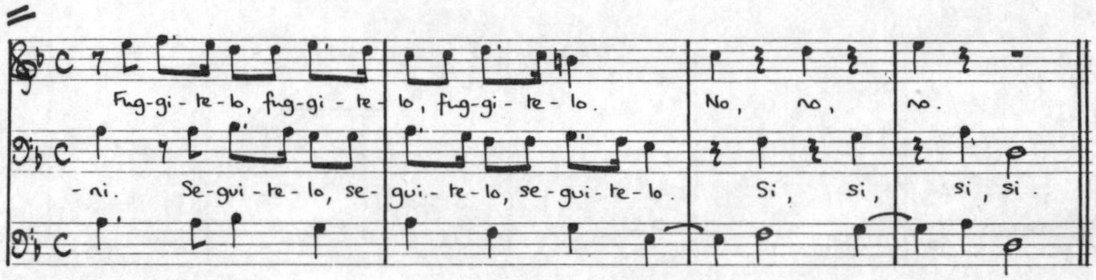

Similar treatment occurs in *Scipione Affricano* (III.4) with Ericlea and Scipione, and in *Elena*(II.6) with Menelao and Peritoo. This idea was even extended to a trio in *Rosinda* (III.11) where two characters, Aurilla and Vafrillo, express mutual love, with the third (Rudione) left out; and there is a parallel occurrence in *Eliogabalo* (I.1). This dramatic situation, which was so much enhanced by the music, anticipates that of the canonic quartet in *Cosi fan tutte*.

Most subtle of all, perhaps, is the occasion in *Eritrea* (I.8) when two characters (Laodicea and Theramene) sing the duet 'O luci belle'. Both characters are singing to a third, Eritrea herself, who is disguised as her dead brother Periandro and 'married' to Laodicea. Laodicea sings to Eritrea in an appeal for more marital attention, while Theramene, deluded, sings to what he believes to be the image of his dead lover.

Larger ensembles than duets are comparatively rare in Cavalli's operas, and generally occur only at conclusions as already observed. But occasionally Cavalli could employ an ensemble for a dramatic purpose. In *Eritrea* (I.9), a scene of much agitated recitative where a messenger announces the arrest of one of the chief characters, four of the others sing the brief quartet 'O luminoso apunto'. The captured prince duly arrives in the following scene, so this isolated moment of ensemble-singing neatly separates two recitative scenes. It also serves the purpose of uniting the four characters as they express the one sentiment upon which they are in total agreement: the belief that their difficulties will now be resolved. (In this respect it is not unlike the quartet in *Idomeneo,* where the four characters are singing separately of their own individual miseries, and come together only on the word 'soffrir').

Cavalli's natural dramatic inventiveness, then, ensures that at the peak of his own operatic composition (about 1645 to 1665) he could use aria and closed form for all dramatic purposes. But, like all his contemporaries, he began to feel subtle changes of operatic emphasis during the late 1650's and 1660's. First, as Italy's most celebrated singers became ever more popular, audiences began to idolise and lionise them, and to demand more opportunities for display of their purely technical and virtuoso talents. This meant that composers were pressurised into meeting these demands for extra arias. The printed *scenario* to the libretto of *Erismena* indicates that arias are now included as much for their own musical interest as for any enhancement of dramatic situation. It contains many descriptions such as 'Erismena rimasta sola canta una Aria sopra la Speranza, e si parte', which manifestly reveals a change in the whole aesthetic of opera. Secondly, the more formal types of ABA and ABB form began to become more complex, and the fluent and malleable through-composed form was gradually abandoned in their favour. The aria 'O care effigi' from *Erismena* is in an ABCCA form, which is an extension of ABA. P.A. Ziani's *Le Fortune di Rodope e di Damira* of the following year has an aria, 'Voglio un giorno inamorarmi', in an ABBCDD, or a double-ABB, form. At the same time, the element of technical virtuosity was being increased. The aria 'Troppo in alto sete andate' from Ziani's *Annibale* of 1661 opens:

and in the next season Castrovillari's *Cleopatra* contained an astonishing example of advanced coloratura:

So aria was by no means still part of an even musico-dramatic façade, but was clearly beginning to emerge as a dominant feature. Extra, non-dramatic arias were added even during the course of the rehearsal period immediately before production, and many printed librettos of the 1660's and 1670's have addenda giving the texts of last-minute insertions. The librettist Aureli complained bitterly of this practice, which distorted the dramatic flow of his opera, in his preface to *Claudio Cesare* of 1673, and, as we have seen, he even cited the singers themselves as being responsible for these distortions.[17]

This gradual move towards the aria's monopoly of opera, and the consequent breakdown of dramatic fluency, brought about the decline of the art form in the 1660's and 1670's. But it was fortunate for Cavalli that opera had not yet developed into this non-dramatic showcase when he was at his own peak; and it was fortunate for opera that a composer of Cavalli's stature could use emerging forms to such dramatic advantage.

— *Recitative* —

Apart from through-composed or multi-partite arias, where the drama can be seen to be developing through the emotions of the characters (a technique much more akin to *opera seria* than to *opera buffa*), most of the action takes place within the recitative. Cavalli's recitative follows the idealistic principles of the *Camerata*, and sets the text according to its natural rhythms and inflections. Unmeasured recitative is therefore built on a predictable harmonic structure, with melismas on emotional or descriptive words, and cadential clichés. It is important to observe that actual note values at cadences probably have very little significance. Closes should be sung as naturally as the rest of the recitative, and only ornamented where the text or situation permits. This is not clear from the appearance of the scores. Frequently Cavalli writes long notes at cadences, suggesting a need for ornamentation; but at many of them, any hiatus caused by such treatment would be dramatically undesirable. Conversely, there are occasions where the note values are shorter, in keeping with the rest of the recitative, yet seem to require ornamentation. Cavalli's inconsistency here can perhaps be accounted for by the speed at which he wrote his operas. The familiar notational patterns that he so hastily and automatically adopted should therefore be treated with caution in performance, for their execution rarely bears relation to

First page of Cavalli's autograph score of *Rosinda*, 1651 *(Reproduced by permission of the Biblioteca Marciana, Venice)*

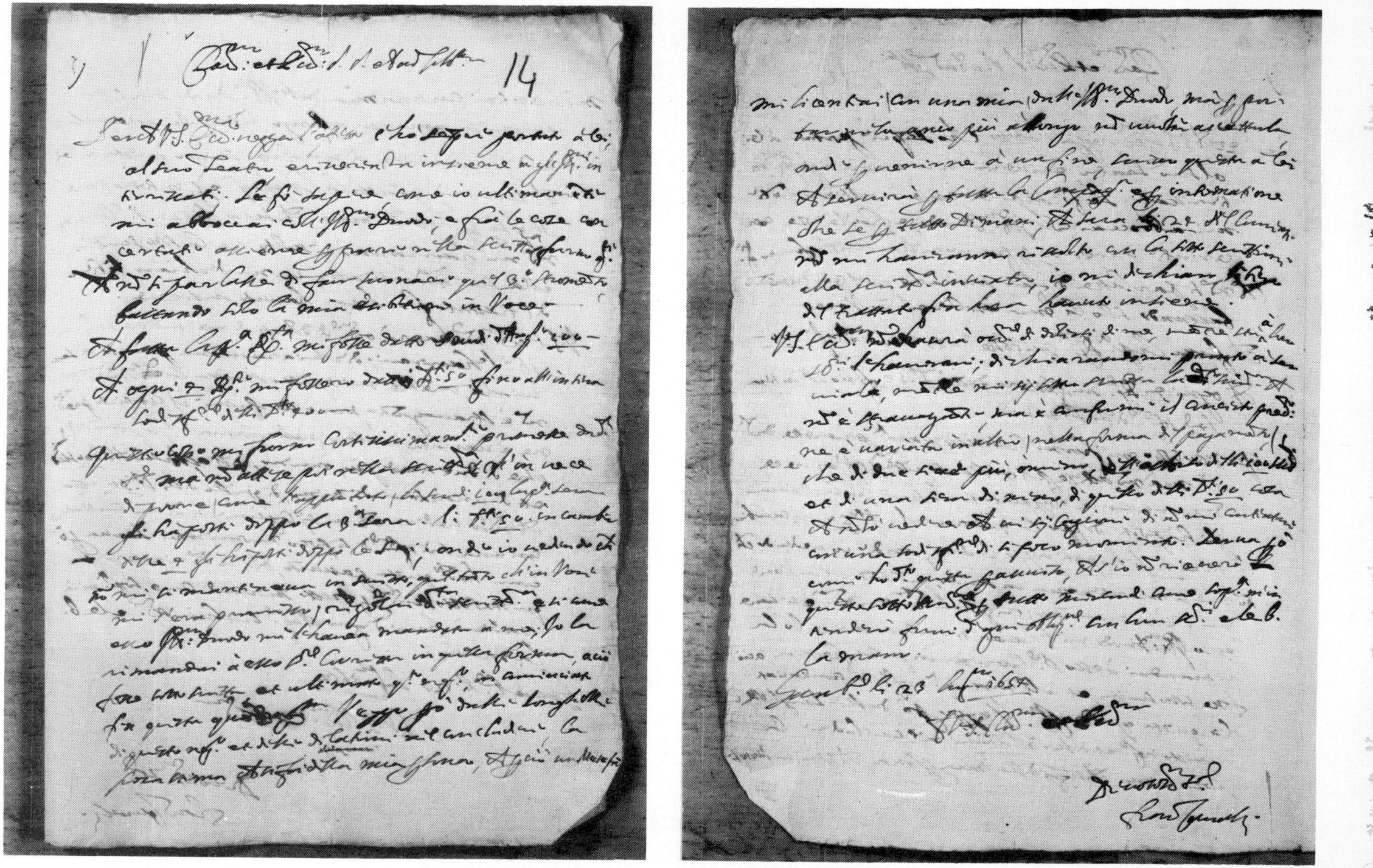

Letter from Cavalli to Marco Faustini, 1654. (See Appendix III, iv.)
(Reproduced by permission of the Archivio di Stato, Venice)

TENORE Primo Choro

MVSICHE SACRE

CONCERNENTI

Messa, e Salmi Concertati con Istromenti Imni Antifone & Sonate, A Due, 3. 4. 5. 6. 8. 10. e 12. Voci

DI

FRANCESCO CAVALLI

Organista Della Serenissima Republica, in S. Marco.

CONSACRATE

AL SERENISSIMO

GIO CARLO

CARDINAL, DE MEDICI

CON PRIVILGIO

IN VENETIA C

Appresso Alessandro Vincenti MDC LVI.

Title page of Cavalli's major publication of sacred music, *Musiche Sacre*, 1656
(Reproduced by permission of the Conservatorio G.B. Martini, Bologna)

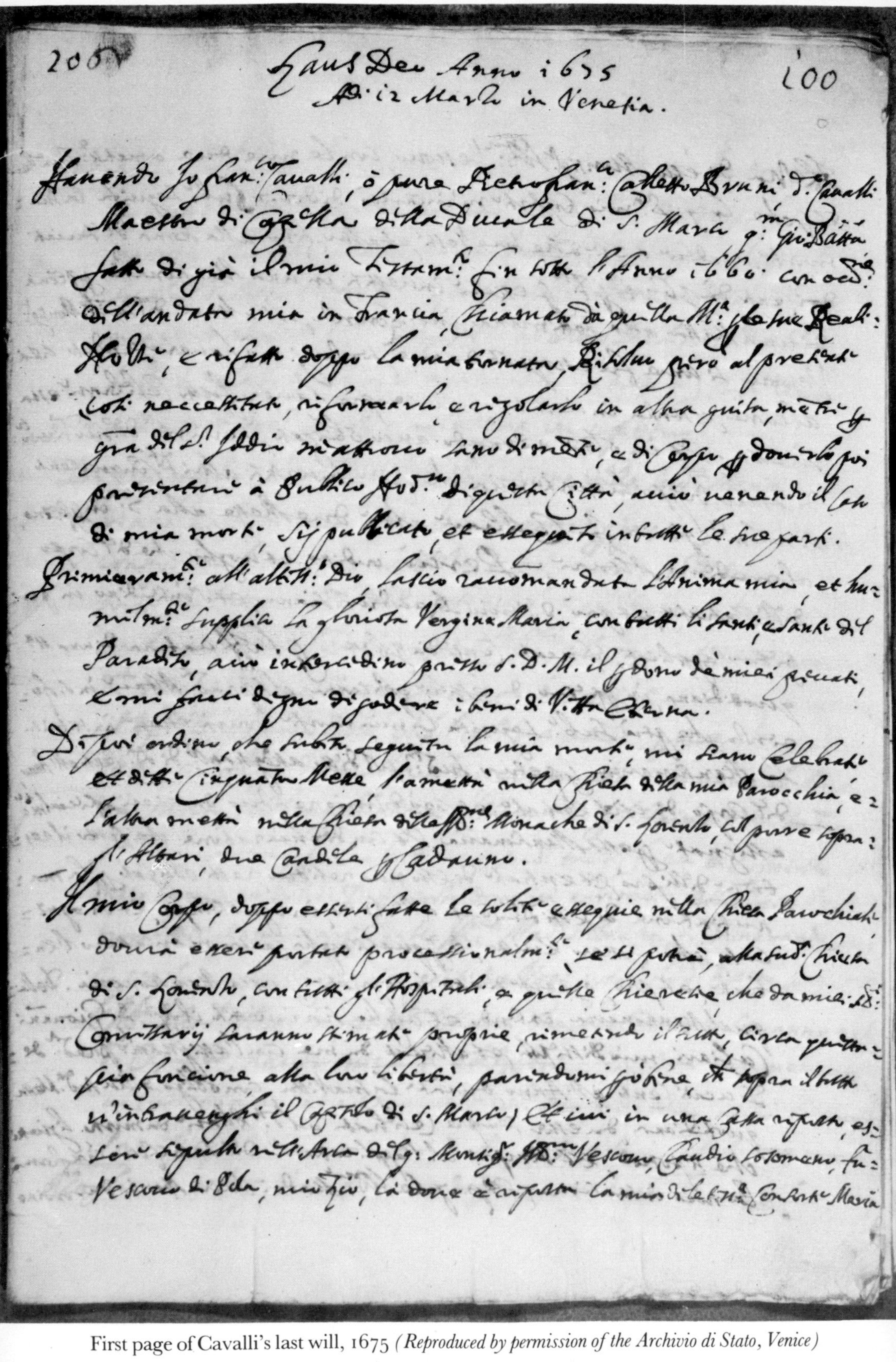
205 Laus Deo Anno 1675 100
Adì 12 Marzo in Venetia.

Havendo io Fran.co Cavalli, ò pure Pietro Fran.co Caletti Bruni d.o Cavalli
Maestro di Capella della Ducale di S. Marco q.m Gio: Batta
fatto di già il mio Testam.to fin sotto l'Anno 1660 con occ.ne
dell'andata mia in Francia, chiamato da quella M.tà per le sue Reali
Nozze, e rifatto doppo la mia tornata, Ritrovo però al present.e
tal necessità, riformarlo, e rigolarlo in altra guisa, mentre p.
gra del S. Iddio mi attrovo sano di ment.e, e di Corpo, p. dovendolo poi
presentarsi à publico Nod.ro di questa Città, acciò venendo il caso
di mia mort.e sij publicato, et esseguito in tutte le sue parti.
Primieram.te all'Altiss.o Dio lascio raccomandata l'Anima mia, et hu=
milm.te supplico la gloriosa Vergine Maria, con tutti li Santi, e Sante del
Paradiso, acciò intercedino presso S. D. M. il perdono de miei peccati,
e mi facci degno di godere i beni di Vita Eterna.
Di poi ordino, che subito seguita la mia morte, mi siano Celebrat.e
Cinquanta Messe l'ametà nella Chiesa della mia Parocchia, e
l'altra metà nella Chiesa delle RR.de Monache di S. Lorenzo, et pure sopra
gl'Altari due Candele p. Cadauno.
Il mio Corpo, doppo essersi fatte le solit.e esequie nella Chiesa Parochial.e
doverà esser portato processionalm.te, se si potrà, alla sud.a Chiesa
di S. Lorenzo, con tutti gl'Hospitali, e quelle Chieresie che da mia
Commissarij saranno stimat.e proprie, rimettendo il tutto, circa questa
sua funcione alla loro libertà, parendomi però, che sopra il tutto
v'intervenghi il Capitolo di S. Marco, et ivi in una Cassa riposto, es=
ser sepolto nell'Arca dell'q. Monsig.r Ill.mo Vescovo Claudio Sosomeno, fu
Vescovo di Pola, mio zio, là dove è sepolta la mia dilett.ma Consort.e Maria

First page of Cavalli's last will, 1675 *(Reproduced by permission of the Archivio di Stato, Venice)*

the actual value of the written notes. Only when there is a rhythmic connection between the voice and the bass line should the cadence be performed in strict time. The Prologue to *Doriclea* exemplifies this, where the bass line imitates the last vocal melisma:

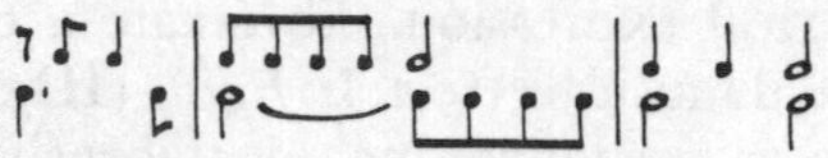

Very occasionally, Cavalli himself supplies the cadence with ornamentation, as for example in *Pompeo Magno* (I.2):

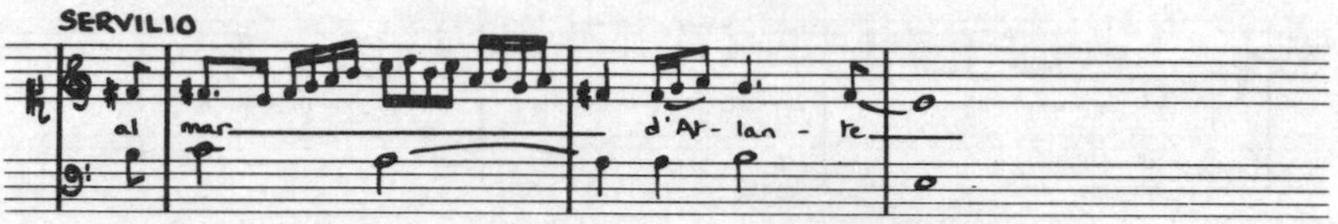

Otherwise, ornamentation should be applied in places where it would not be destructive of dramatic fluency, and the musical phrase should be brought to a full close as naturally as possible.[18]

A melodic, rather than rhythmic, cadence technique is to flatten the third in a major key immediately before the close. This occurs quite frequently throughout the operas, and is as much used in aria as in recitative; but its effect is no less startling for being slightly familiar. Thisandro's mournful recitative in *Rosinda* (II.11) illustrates this:

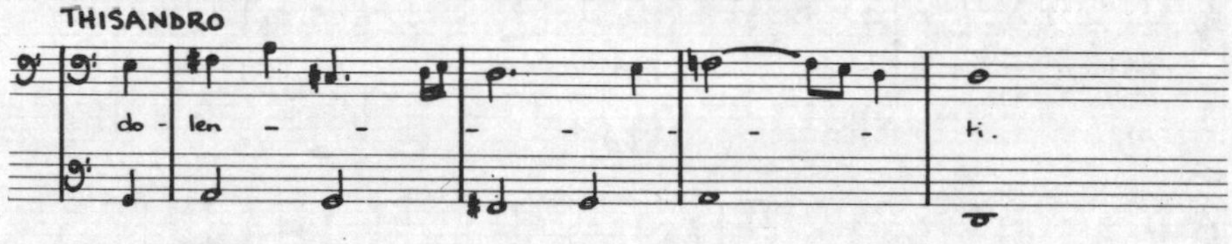

Rosinda (I.2) also has one extraordinary instance of a sharpened third in a minor key—a complete reversal of the more common practice. Here again it is obviously the text which has inspired this move in Cavalli's mind.

Harmonically, the recitative is generally straightforward. But at moments of great tension, or strong drama, Cavalli departs into strange and unrelated flat keys, with superb dramatic results. These moments perhaps contribute to the insecure tonal structure of Cavalli's general musical style, but also agains illustrate his immense capacity for theatrical expression. To create a dramatic effect, he produces an unusual musical effect. In *Egisto* (III.5) Egisto's solo mad scene, set entirely as recitative, includes abrasive dissonances and wide leaps, as Cavalli musically portrays Egisto's insanity. Such graphic illustration perhaps equals Handel in its dramatic power.

There are also occasional clashes between the sharpened and unsharpened versions of the same note, rather as in sixteenth-century English church music. Again the musical effect considerably heightens the dramatic impact. In *Orione* (II.10) Diana's soliloquy contains the following cadence:

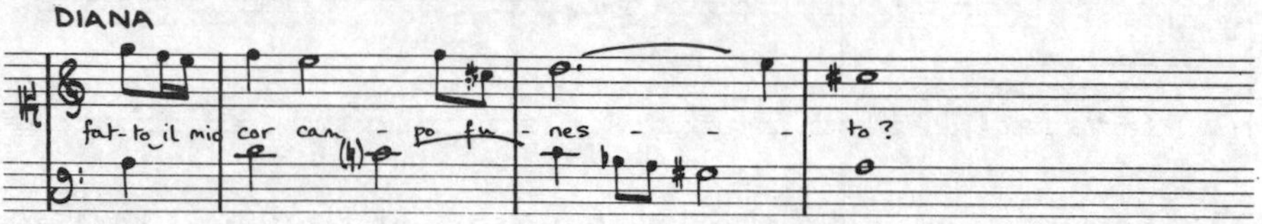

It has already been shown that Cavalli could very easily slip from recitative into measured music for a few bars, if inspired by the text, of which such passages were essentially illustrative embellishments. It was also possible to lend a slight structural basis to recitative without going into a strict tempo, but by using the bass line in a particular way. It could move in a circle of fifths, or by step, or be centred round a particular key, or even descend a complete chromatic scale. This was generally employed at highly dramatic points. In *Erismena* (II.5) Erismena recognises her former lover as he tries to poison her:

and in *Scipione Affricano* (III.2) Ericlea's recitative is neatly incorporated over an ascending and descending scale:

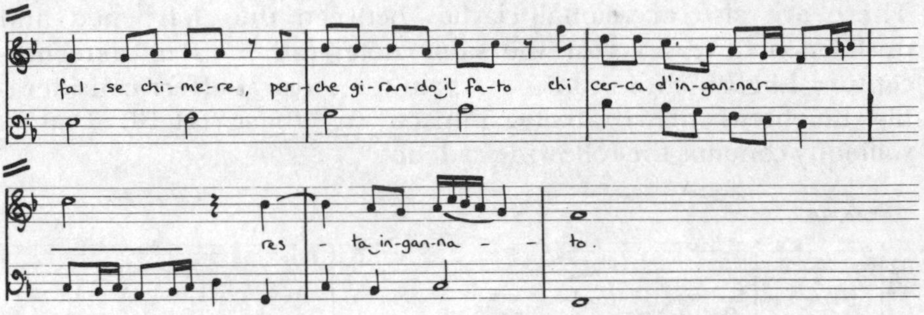

The bass pattern could also be some sort of sequence. In *Xerse* (I.16) the quick conversation between Clito and Amastre is united by a descending pattern:

Such organisation of the bass line was always prompted by the text; and the incorporation of scales or sequences served to intensify the accumulation or release of tension (as in *Erismena* and *Scipio Affricano*), or to give shape and regularity to a rapid eachange of dialogue (as in *Xerse*).

With the later librettos of Aureli and Minato, dialogue became much more realistically conversational. There are some superb scenes where the recitative is rapidly exchanged, producing fine dramatic effect. Cavalli rose instinctively to such passages, and served the dialogue with a fast and simple recitative style, as for example in *Xerse* (I.5):

One of Cavalli's finest musical techniques was his use of accompanied recitative. This was a comparatively regular feature from the 1640's onwards for moments of climax or tension, and is perhaps the true fulfilment of the old principles of *stile recitativo.* The text is still set at speech rhythm, but the addition of string parts removes the particular passage on to a different musical plane. (Bach employed the same technique with Christus in his setting of the St Matthew Passion.) In Doriclea's solo scene (*Doriclea* III.1) her extensive recitative after the lament breaks periodically into accompanied sections. In *Rosinda* (I.7) Nerea's plea to Pluto is entirely accompanied, and bound by a ritornello; and in *Ipermestra* (I.11) Ipermestra's soliloquy, of a repeated pattern of recitative and aria, is accompanied throughout. One of the most dramatic of all Cavalli's uses of accompanied recitative occurs in *Eritrea* (III.10) when the servant Misena reports to the king how the supposed Periandro is believed to have died. When she repeats Periandro's 'dying words', the delicate melodrama of the situation is richly enhanced by the addition of sustained string parts.

Passages of affective recitative, with or without accompaniment, were given to none but serious characters. (The above example from *Eritrea* is a mild exception, but Misena is quoting the speech of a major character.) It would seem therefore that one line of development of these recitatives was into the through-composed aria, which was similarly able to trace the development of a character's thoughts through a piece. As it has been observed, the through-composed aria gradually became more formalised and sectionalised, and it is possible to follow how recitative yielded its moments of high drama to the aria before aria itself became overblown at the expense of dramatic fluency.

— *Characterisation* —

Cavalli's musical characterisation is fairly consistent throughout all 27 works. Generally the serious characters are less strongly drawn than their servants, who show *commedia dell'arte* derivations and therefore fall into specific types. There are old nurses (*sibille vecchie*); young confidantes to the main female characters (*soubrette*); buffo comic servants, often with marked bibulous tendencies (Scapino and Harlequin); and young pages (Pedrolino). All these four types appear regularly throughout Cavalli's composition period, as the following table shows:

		NURSES	CONFIDANTES	BUFFO SVTS	PAGES
1640	*Apollo*	Cirilla [a]			
1642	*La Virtù*			Erino [s]	
1643	*Egisto*	Dema [s]			
1644	*Ormindo*	Erice [a]			Nerillo
1645	*Doriclea*		Melloe	Orindo [s]	
1649	*Giasone*	Delfa [a]	Alinda	Demo [t]	
1650	*Orimonte*	Alcea [s]		Lisi [t]	
1651	*Oristeo*			Oresde [a]	Ermino
	Rosinda		Cillena	Rudinoe [ab]	Vafrillo
1652	*Calisto*		Linfea		
	Eristrea		Misena		Lesbo
1653	*Veremonda*	Zaida [s]	Vespina	D. Buscon [t]	
1654	*Ipermestra*		Elisa		Alindo
1655	*Xerse*			Elviro [a]	Clito
1656	*Statira*			Indiano [t]	
	Erismena	Alcesta [a]	Florida	Argippo [bar]	
1657	*Artemisia*	Erisbe [a]			Eurillo
1660	*Elena*			Iro [t]	
1662	*Ercole*				paggio
1664	*Scipione*	Ceffea [t]		Lesbo [bar]	
1665	*Muzio*	Porfiria [t]	Harpalia		Milo
	Ciro (rev.)			Delfido [a]	Euretto
1666	*Pompeo*	Atrea [t]		Delfo [a]	Servilio
1668	*Eliogabalo*				
1670	*Erismena* II	Alcesta [t]		Argippo [a]	

s = soprano, a = tenor, bar = baritone, b = bass

These comic figures comment on the main action, and are also involved in their own subplots, invariably based on some amorous entanglement. Sometimes their music appears clumsy, which perhaps implies conscious characterisation on the part of Cavalli. The entry of the elderly nurse Porfiria in *Muzio Scevola* (I.9), for example, shows a remarkable lack of rhythmic or harmonic centre. Had Cavalli momentarily lost concentration, or was he deliberately suggesting a doddering old woman?

Pages and *damigelle* generally have the most lighthearted music, and it would often seem that their inclusion was as much for musical as dramatic contrast. The *paggio* in *Ercole Amante*, for example, always sings over a light moving bass in crotchet rhythm. Eurillo in *Artemisia* is in fact the court page-musician, providing a constant excuse for tuneful arias, such as in the first scene of the opera, when Artemisia calls him with the request 'Al mio defonto prega pace col canto', and he duly sings her a cheering aria.

The serious characters are less vividly drawn, and there is less immediate differentiation between them. If anything, the women are stronger than the men, both musically and dramatically. Their parts are bigger and their music better, indicating the greater popularity of female singers in the period immediately before the ascendancy of the castrato. It is generally the women who are in disguise as warriors (already a much stronger dramatic concept than a man disguised as a serving-maid), and they are determined to brave all kinds of political and military dangers when pursuing matters of the heart. On the other hand, the men are remarkably inactive, mostly singing arias about love and occasionally being moved to jealous fury. Even in the heavily historical librettos, centred round important military characters, like *Xerse, Scipione Affricano, Muzio Scevola* and *Pompeo Magno*, the martial qualities and activities of these heroes are completely subordinated to the actions of their ladies.

It is interesting that most characters in every plot are at some time allowed to appear sympathetic. However relevant or irrelevant a character may be in the action, or however vindictive his role in the overall dramatic outline, he will generally be given a solo scene in which he soliloquises on his own predicament and sings a memorable and effective aria. Not all these solo scenes were planned in the libretto. In *Xerse* the not inconsiderable role of Adelanta is ultimately irrelevant in that her ardent passion for Arsamene is never reciprocated and so she does not participate in the final quartet; she merely confuses all issues until the denouement. Yet in the second act (scene 13) she has a solo scene of effective recitative, and a glorious string-accompanied aria with pathetic cadences, which is doubtless the highlight of the role. The text for this section does not appear in the printed libretto, and from the appearance of the score it has been inserted after the main part of the composition. The original Adelanta presumably insisted on having a more prominent, and less villainous, role. There are several other instances of this 'spotlight' technique for sub-principals, and therefore very few characters who remain unsympathetic throughout. Only Pirro in *Didone*, Ericlea in *La Virtù de' strali d'Amore* and Ismeno in *Muzio Scevola* have no chance to play to the audience.

It is extremely rare for a serious character not to achieve his or her desire. But *Calisto*, a somewhat unusual opera in most respects, does contain such an instance in the character of Giunone. At the end of the opera Giunone is avenged by not contented—an unfamiliar condition for a Venetian opera of this period. It is in fact a dramatic syndrome that she shares only with characters like Ottavia in Monteverdi's *Poppea*.

Particularly during the complex central period of the 1650's, characters frequently go into disguise for part or all of the opera. Both dramatically and musically, such a technique provides excellent opportunities for double-characterisation, as the audience sees the person in both roles. A disguised princess generally has occasion in solo scenes to express the difficulties of duplicity, and the situations in which she finds herself (particularly that of being attractive to women when in male guise) are almost Shakespearian. Indeed, Viola's soliloquy from *Twelfth Night* (II.2) might well echo the thoughs of Eritrea or Erismena:

> Disguise, I see, thou art a wickedness
> Wherein the pregnant enemy does much.

How easy is it for the proper-false
In women's waxen hearts to set their forms!
Alas, our frailty is the cause, not we;
For such as we are made of, such we be.

———

O time, thou must untangle this, not I;
It is too hard a knot for me to untie.

When characters go into disguise during the course of an opera, and become recognisably different people, they frequently adopt different clefs and registers. In *Calisto* Giove disguises himself as Diana and sings in the soprano register instead of the bass. Similarly in *Le Nozze di Teti e di Peleo* Discordia temporarily disguises herself as Nereo in order to confuse the main plot, and becomes a tenor instead of an alto. At this point the score refers to Discordia as 'in habito e voce di Nereo'. This means that a character in disguise would be sung by the person whose physique he was temporarily borrowing, and not by the original singer.

— *Orchestra* —

In all Cavalli's scores, whether autograph or not, the area where the most ambiguities arise and remain unexplained is the orchestra.[19] The size of the orchestra in Venetian opera houses has very much been questioned in present-day research, with different editors and conductors producing very different results. The confusion arises initially from the apparent inconsistency in the scores as to the use of a five-part or a three-part string texture. Of Cavalli's 28 extant scores, eleven have a five-part texture, five a four-part texture, and twelve a three-part texture, as follows.

	5-part	4-part	3-part
1639	*Teti e Peleo*		
1640		*Apollo e Dafne*	
1641	*Didone*		
1642	*La Virtù*		
1643	*Egisto*		
1644	*Ormindo*		

	5-part	4-part	3-part
1645	*Doriclea*		
1649	*Giasone*		
1650			*Orimonte*
1651			*Oristeo*
1651			*Rosinda*
1652		*Calisto*	
1652			*Eritrea*
1653			*Orione*
1653			*Veremonda*
1654			*Ipermestra*
1655			*Xerse*
1656			*Statira*
1656			*Erismena* I
1657			*Artemisia*
1660		*Elena*	
1662	*Ercole Amante*		
1664	*Scipione*		
1665	*Muzio*		
1665	*Ciro* (rev.)		
1666	*Pompeo*		
1668		*Eliogabalo*	
1670			*Erismena* II

It would seem that the size of the orchestra was determined first by the size of the theatre, and secondly by the actual date. All six operas written for the small Teatro Sant'Apollinare (including Ziani's *Le Fortune di Rodope e di Damira*) call for the small three-part band, with the exception of *Calisto* which occasionally employs an extra viola. Conversely, of the nine operas presented at the much larger Teatro San Cassiano, seven have five-part strings, as have both operas for San Salvatore. The size of the theatre is therefore a useful starting criterion for fixing the size of the orchestra. What emerges even more clearly is that the three-part scores are consistently within the 1650's, whether for the Teatro Sant'Apollinare or not. The smaller band therefore appears in *Xerse* for SS. Giovanni e Paolo, and even more surprisingly in *Ipermestra* for the grand Florentine celebrations. Such vertical contraction of orchestral texture is consistent with the move towards greater intimacy in the size of casts and in actual plots. There were smaller numbers of characters in the 1650's than in the 1660's, and the chorus was employed less spectacularly. The vast scale of, for example, *Teti e Peleo* (1639) with 28 characters, or *Didone* (1641) with 24 characters, was gradually reduced over the years, so that *Giasone* (1649) had sixteen, *Rosinda* (1651) eleven, *Erismena* (1656) ten, and *Artemisia* (1657) nine. After Cavalli's visit to France at the turn of the decade, taste began to swing back towards a larger scale: the three consecutive historical operas, *Scipione Affricano, Muzio Scevola* and *Pompeo Magno* (1664, 1665 and 1666) have 15 or 16 characters, and huge choruses in crowds and ballets.

These considerations account for any appearance of inconsistency which may be obtained from superficial study of Cavalli's scores, leading to the misconception that a five-part texture should be used constantly. Above all, it is the music itself which is in every way adequate and complete. In *Rosinda* (I.8) for example, Nerea's aria 'Qui dove inonda il pianto ogni sponda' goes into quadruple time. Here the tight succession of contrapuntal entries between the basso continuo, voice and the two violin parts shows that there is no room for alteration or expansion, which in these smaller textures are therefore neither necessary nor desirable:

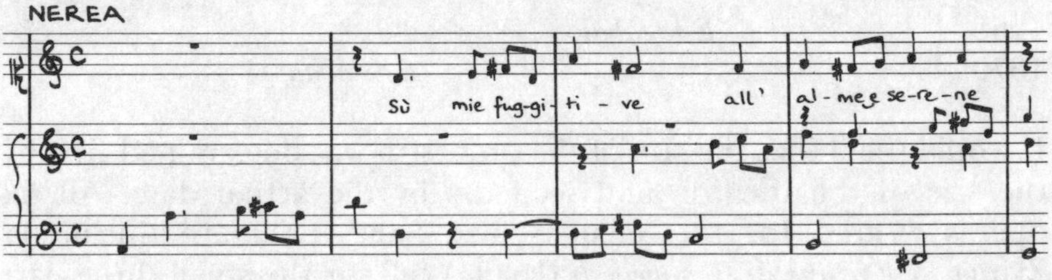

The orchestral payment records survive from two of Cavalli's operas: *Antioco* in 1659 and the revival of *Ciro* in 1665.[20] The records indicate that each string part was played on a single instrument, and that this basic string texture was supported by two or three harpsichords and two theorboes. The orchestra was used for opening sinfonias, ritornellos to arias or between scenes, and occasionally for accompanying arias and recitative. At many places in Cavalli's scores there are blank staves over the vocal line, indicating that upper string parts are to be added. In the case of a strophic form, accompaniment is not always written out after the first stanza, but its repetition is still intended, as shown by an aria for Virtù, 'Son pur', in the *Doriclea* prologue. At the beginning of the second stanza there is the dircction '2ª stroffa con li istessi instromenti'. Close study of accompanied arias, or arias where strings intermittently appear, suggests that upper parts should occasionally be added also where there is little or no indication in the score. Rather few arias are actually accompanied throughout; most often the strings only appear between the vocal entries of the aria, and perhaps join with the voice for the last few bars before the cadence. This practice may well be one borrowed from contemporary sacred music, for the strings and voice alternate in the manner of antiphonal choirs. It is therefore likely that strings should similarly be added where there are gaps between the vocal entries.[21] In performance it has certainly been shown that without these interludes the impetus of the aria is considerably impaired.

No complete orchestral parts survive from the original productions, but it does seem that in any case they were very haphazardly made. An instrumental part for each individual musical number in which an instrument was involved was apparently written on a separate sheet of paper. In *Artemisia* (II.6) Cavalli set the aria 'Di trombe guerriere' twice, the second time on the back of a hastily-taken sheet of paper which was then inserted into the main score. This sheet (f.59) is a page of a string part in an alto clef. The textual incipit at the beginning of the music identifies this as belonging to the opening speech 'Dure selve' of the whole work. The potential chaos in the orchestral pit during performances is horrifying to contemplate.[22]

The derivations of the terms 'sinfonia' and 'ritornello' were originally straightforward and specific. A sinfonia was an instrumental item which either introduced an act or was played between scenes. A ritornello was attached to an aria or other closed form, and it certainly returned at the end or in between stanzas. Composers did however become somewhat casual in their labelling of such pieces, and by the 1650's the terms were used almost interchangeably. Ritornellos are usually based on the arias they follow, and even occasionally on recitative. The sinfonia at the beginning of each opera is generally bipartite, with a slow, broad $\frac{4}{2}$ section followed by a faster section in triple or quadruple time. Occasionally the two sections use identical musical material differentiated only by the rhythm and speed of performance, almost in the manner of a Pavane and Galliard. The introduction to *Rosinda* illustrates this:

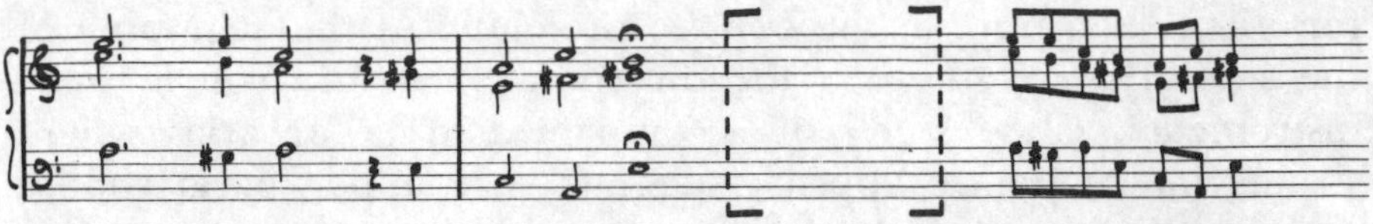

Sinfonias between scenes are no doubt intended to allow time for set-changes, a technicality Cavalli felt obliged to point out to the French performers in his carefully-marked score of *Ercole Amante* (V.1/2: 'Questa sinf [a] si fà per aspettare la mutatione della Scena').

As well as the small string band with its continuo section of harpsichords and theorboes, brass instruments also were occasionally introduced. The libretto to *Le Nozze di Teti e di Peleo* opens with the following direction: 'La Fama suona la Tromba, di poi dà principio al Canto', although no music for this trumpet-call exists in the extant score. In the same work, the opening scene in Hades includes the recitative text:

> Già divulgar sù le tremende Arene
> Il Concilio Infernal trombe tonanti
> — — —
> A svegliar dunque i sonnachiosi Dei
> Gonfiate, ò negri Avaldi
> In fieri carmi orribili metalli.

This is followed by a *chiamata*:

In the following scene (on the 'Lido Marino') there is the 'chiamata alla caccia', also in $\frac{12}{8}$, and in scene 4 of the same act the text refers to 'corni, tamburi c trombc'. Thc Prologuc to *Rosinda* has thc direction 'chiamata de la magica tromba'; a declaration of enemy surrender in *Erismena* (I.14) is heralded by trumpets; *Artemisia* (II.6) has an aria 'Di trombe guerriere' in C major with trumpets throughout; and there are two similar appearances in *Elena*. The first (I.10) is a brief four-bar section called 'lotta' and accompanies a fight, and the second (II.16) is called 'tocco'. This term became used with increasing frequency in the operas of the 1660's and 1670's (for example *Pompeo Magno*), when it seems that trumpets were assuming a more regular position actually in the pit. But all earlier examples suggest that they were either specific stage props, or else played on stage to enhance a particular dramatic moment. There is however a possible second function for the trumpets. It had apparently always been the custom of the court operas in Florence and Mantua to herald the beginning of an opera with a brass fanfare or toccata (for example that printed in Monteverdi's *Orfeo*). The above-quoted direction before the Prologue of *Teti e Peleo* suggests that this feature was also adopted in early Venetian operas. Although there is no further evidence of this practice in the 1640's and 1650's, there are indications that it returned in the 1660's. The English traveller Sir Philip Skippon reveals that a trumpet call was used at the beginning of the evening's entertainment in 1664, for he observed:[23]

> Before the curtain was drawn up, a trumpet sounded, and a violin answered it very well. . . . We saw another play (at Grimani's theatre) called Scipius Africanus. Before they began, the trumpet and violin play'd.

Two of the operas that he saw, *Rosilena* and *Achille,* do not survive, nor does the score of the third, *Scipione Affricano,* show any indication of such an opening to the opera. But P.A. Ziani's *Candaule* of 1680[24] opens in the following way:

which seems to be exactly what Skippon had heard. While the precise nature of these trumpet pieces is therefore obscure, it does seem likely that their use, first out of the pit and then in it, was more extensive than the scores reveal.

— *Chorus* —

Just as an analysis of orchestral texture in Cavalli's scores reveals a general thinning out in the 1650's, so does a similar analysis of choruses. Taken chronologically, choruses appear as follows:

1639	*Teti e Peleo*	SSA/SSATTB/SSATTB/SSA
1640	*Apollo e Dafne*	SATB/SSAT
1641	*Didone*	ATTB/SSATTB
1642	*La Virtù*	SSA/SSMSA/SSAT
1643	*Egisto*	SSSA
1644	*Ormindo*	TTB
1645	*Doriclea*	TTB/SSSA/B
1649	*Giasone*	ATTB/ATTB
1650	*Orimonte*	SSA
1651	*Oristeo*	T
1651	*Rosinda*	STB/S
1652	*Calisto*	S/SATB
1652	*Eritrea*	—
1653	*Orione*	—
1653	*Veremonda*	—
1654	*Ipermestra*	SSATTB/S/ATB/ATB

1655	*Xerse*	SATB/SAT
1656	*Statira*	—
1656	*Erismena*	—
1657	*Artemisia*	—
1660	*Elena*	SAT/TB
1662	*Ercole Amante*	SSA/SATB/SATB/SSA
1664	*Scipione*	SSA/SATB
1665	*Muzio*	SATB
1665	*Ciro* (revival)	SATB
1666	*Pompeo*	SATB
1668	*Eliogabalo*	ATB/SATB

Again there is a marked symmetrical pattern. The grand chorus effects of the earliest operas were no doubt taken over from the operas of Florence and Rome. As the essential qualities of the Venetian form of opera became more clearly defined, and its creators concentrated more on entangled relationships within a small group of people, so the need for the chorus decreased. It became smaller, and in the 1650's it vanished almost completely. *Ipermestra* for Florence and *Ercole Amante* for Paris once more threw the emphasis on grand spectacular presentations with chorus and ballet; otherwise only *Xerse* and *Elena* used very modest choral resources. With the move towards the more spectacular historical librettos in the 1660's, choruses were once more adopted. Yet it would seem that their chief contribution was essentially visual rather than musical. Chorus music was generally short and simple, whether in six parts or two, and the choristers were employed probably as much for spectacular as for musical interest. As Skippon again observed at *Scipione Affricano,* the visual impact of large numbers of people on stage at the beginning of an opera was considerable:[25]

> . . . the curtain was drawn up, and there appear'd a magnificent scene, representing an amphitheatre fill'd with spectators; and at the further end sat *Scipio Africanus* in his triumphant chair, before whom gladiators danced, and fought very well.

During the 1650's however, Cavalli's operas concentrated on complexity within a small compass, and the grand scenic effects produced by choruses temporarily became redundant.

— *Performance practice* —

Cavalli worked under constant pressure to get his new operas into the rehearsal stages and then to performance. It is relevant therefore to summarise briefly the processes involved, using evidence supplied, if not from the composer himself, from his immediate contemporaries.

The composition and preparation of a new work appears always to have been done at speed. Most librettists make excuses for the deficiencies in their work by protesting that it was all done against time, and certain facts substantiate this. P.A. Ziani twice made the remarkable statement that his *Annibale* had been written in five days, a claim that Beregan's libretto seems to support.[26] He asserts that the whole preparation of the opera took only 20 days, and he asks for the audience's sympathy for the pressures of time that the company has had to endure.[27] Certainly the libretto was in the hands of the composer as soon as it was written. In his apology for haste in the libretto to *Euridamante* (1654),[28] the librettist Giacomo dall'Angelo states that his text had no sooner been completed than it was being set to music.[29] A further letter from Ziani reveals that a composer could produce the score in stages,[30] and this is also implied by letters from Cesti in Innsbruck.[31]

During the rehearsal period, which probably lasted about six weeks,[32] alterations were made in both the libretto and the score, and in *La Costanza di Rosmonda* (1660)[33] Aureli emphasises that these changes were made right up to the final rehearsals.[34] His *Amore infruttuose di Pirro* of the following year[35] shows that when a particularly fine singer suddenly became available the opera was re-arranged at the last minute in order to accommodate him into the cast. In a stop-press addition, he states that a certain Signor Clemente arrived in Venice after the opera had been cast, but in order not to deprive Venetian audiences of so distinguished a singer, the opera had been altered to include him.[36] Apart from the ballos and intermedio-type movements between the acts, which were of the most transitory nature and have very rarely survived, the Prologues seem to be the last sections to be written and rehearsed. The libretto to Apolloni's *Argia* (1670)[37] shows that with this opera the Prologue (printed at the end of the text) was thrown together at the last possible minute, using arias from other operas. This fascinating Prologue shows Apollo, Piacere and three Muses in a library, from whose shelves they remove scores and sing arias from them. Between the sections of recitative there are the following directions:

Qui si canta un' Aria dell'Ipermestra[38]

———

Qui si canta un' Aria del Fabio Massimo[39]

———

Qui si canta un' Arietta del Ratto delle Sabine[40]

———

Qui si canta un'altra Arietta del Ratto delle Sabine

Here the use of recognisable arias from identified operas is an intriguing precursor of *Don Giovanni*.

Instrumental music was also often composed comparatively late, for this would not be needed during the first stages of rehearsal. Many gaps and unrealised ritornellos in the extant scores show this. Very few scores give a sinfonia at the beginning of each act; most of them plunge straight into the vocal material, whether aria or recitative. But it seems likely that there was some sort of brief instrumental introduction before the rise of the curtain. The third act to Cavalli's *Scipione Affricano* shows a particular need for some such prelude, for its opening aria, Ericlea's 'Chi si rende à una bellezza', begins with the voice unaccompanied for two bars before the *basso continuo* enters in imitation:

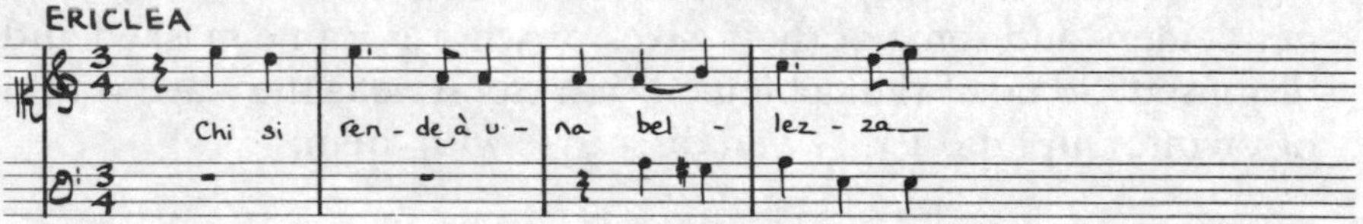

Cavalli's score of *Rosinda* perhaps provides the clue to common practice. Here the bass line to the opening sinfonia of the whole opera is given at the beginning of the other two acts, suggesting that, in the absence of new sinfonias for Acts II and III, the original one from the first act should be repeated.

It is not known precisely how many performances an opera received in one season; but the contract between Cavalli and Marco Faustini in 1658 implies that there could be as many as 26.[41] During the run of an opera some changes could still be made.

Alterations to the part of Endimione in *Calisto* suggest that a second singer took over the role after the production had opened, and the tessitura had to be adapted for him. Since there is no evidence for any revival of *Calisto* these alterations may reasonably be assumed to relate to the original production. Further cuts could even be made. One of the surviving printed librettos of *Eritrea*[42] has cuts marked in ink at several places in the second and third acts. These remove what are essentially superfluities and considerably tighten the construction.

It is finally appropriate to consider briefly how these works were received in their day. Audiences were drawn to opera productions by the reputations of their creators and particularly by those of the participants. Unlike the audiences at productions of straight comedy, those at operas showed a genuine involvement and enthusiasm for the story. Skippon was present at performances of both opera and comedy, and clearly distinguished between two types of audience. At a comedy he observed:[43]

> Before the play began, the gentlemen and company were impatient, and call'd out often *Fuora, fuora;* and they made a great noise when they stamp'd and whistled, and call'd to one another. Those that sat in the boxes did frequently spit upon the company in the pit, so that all appeared very rude. We observed but three acts of the play, which was immodest and obscene; nothing that was sober would please the company, who were ready to hiss, and they disgust anything that was not filthy. The gentlemen, and some of their wives or whores, came masked and disguised. Some of the noblemen that stood near the stage would often interrupt the actors, and discourse with them.

In contrast to this, the audiences at the three operas that he saw were orderly and appreciative:[44]

> When anything pleas'd very well, the company cry'd out, *Bien bien!* The gentlewomen came in masquerade; but when they were in their boxes, they pulled off their vizards: they wear broad falling lace bands. The noblemen were indifferently silent; and those in the boxes did not spit so often in the pit, as they do at the common plays. . . . *Ericlea's* part was acted by her that acted *Rosilena,* who acquitted herself very well, and received

great applause.

It must indeed be remembered that these audiences were entirely responsible for the changes and developments that Cavalli and his contemporaries felt obliged to make. The creators of the art form no doubt shared the sentiment expressed by Samuel Johnson:[45]

> Hard is his lot, that here by Fortune plac'd,
> Must watch the wild Vicissitudes of Taste;
> With ev'ry Meteor of Caprice must play,
> And chase the new-blown Bubbles of our Day.
> Ah! let not Censure term our Fate our Choice,
> The Stage but echoes back the publick Voice.
> The Drama's Laws the Drama's Patrons give,
> For we that live to please, must please to live.

NOTES

1. For a complete catalogue of the Contarini collection, see: T. Wiel: *I codici Musicali Contariniani del secolo XVII nella R. Biblioteca di S. Marco in Venezia* (Venice, 1888).
2. Francesco Contarini, 1623§5; Nicolo Contarini, 1630§2; Carlo Contarini, 1655–6; Domenico Contarini, 1660–74; Luigi Contarini, 1676–83.
3. See P. Camerini: *Piazzola* (Milan, 1925), p.157ff, p.235ff. See also Ivanovich, *op. cit.*, chapter 17 ('Come coll'esempio de' Teatri di Venezia fù aperto il Teatro Contarini con eroica generosità, e magnificenza à Piazzola'), pp.414–420.
4. The works performed at Piazzola were:
   1679 *Le Amazone nelle Isole Fortunate* (Pallavicino–Piccioli)
   1680 *Berenice vendicativa* (Freschi–Rapparini)
   1682 *L'Ermelinda* (Freschi–Piccioli)
   ?1683 *L'Amante muto loquace* (?—Leonardi)
   1684 *L'Erginda* (?—Fontana)
   1685 *Gl'Amori d'Alidaura* (Freschi–Piccioli)
   1686 *L'Odoacre* (?—?)
5. *Toccate e partite d'intavolatura di cimbalo di Gerolamo Frescobaldi* (Rome, 1615). Bnm Mus 69. I am grateful to Thomas Walker for showing me this volume and its inscriptions.
6. *L'orologio del piacere che mostra l'ore del dilettevole soggiorno hauto*

dall'Altezza serenissima d'Ernest Augusto Vesovo d'Osnabruc, Duca di Branswich, Lunebergo, etc. (Piazzola, 1685)

7. The relevant passage is quoted in Wiel, *I codici musicali . . ., op. cit.; Prefazione* vii. This preface also gives a comparatively detailed account of the collection's transition from Piazzola to the Biblioteca Marciana; of which the above description is an approximate précis.

8. Ivanovich, *op. cit.*, p.435.

9. Bnm MS It.IV. 356 (=9880)

10. For example 'Da capo il ritornello' (III.21, f.115); or the more extensive corrections of notes and text in II.2 (f.45ff.)

11. Bnm MS It.IV. 364 (=9888).

12. For these revivals, see Bianconi, 'Caletti', *op. cit.*, p.691. It also seems likely that the surviving score (Bnm MS It.IV. 355 =9879) relates to one of these later productions, for it does not correspond exactly to the original *scenario,* printed in 1642 to coincide with the first Venetian performances. The libretto (not published until 1656) does relate to the score.

13. For a possible explanation of this move, see; E. Rosand: 'Ormindo travestito in Erismena' in *JAMS* XXVIII (1975)

14. For discussions of Cavalli's arias, see: N. Pirrotta: 'Early opera and aria', *op. cit.* B. Hjelmborg: 'Aspects of the aria in the early operas of Cavalli' in *Natalica Musicologica Knud Jeppeson* (Hafniae, 1962), p.173–198. E. Rosand: *Aria in the early operas of Francesco Cavalli* (dissertation, New York University, 1971).

15. For a discussion of the dramatic function of this piece, see: J. Kerman: *Opera as Drama* (New York, 1956), pp.35–6.

16. Eighth book of madrigals, 1638.

17. See Chapter II, p.60, above.

18. For further discussion of this point, see: J.A. Westrup: 'The Cadence in Baroque Recitative' in *Natalica Musicologica Knud Jeppeson* (Hafniae, 1962), pp.243–252.

19. For discussions of the Venetian orchestra, see: D. Arnold: "L'Incoronacione di Poppea' and its orchestral requirements' in *MT* CIV (1963), pp.176–8. J. Beat: 'Monteverdi and the Opera Orchestra of his time' in *The Monteverdi Companion* (ed. D. Arnold and N. Fortune, London, 1968), pp.277–301. R.L. Weaver: 'Orchestration in early Italian opera' in *JAMS* XVII (1964), p.83ff. R. Leppard: 'Cavalli's operas' in *PRMA* XCIII (1967), pp.67§76.

20. ASV, Scuola Grande di S Marco, b.194, A. (unnumbered notebook). Quoted in Arnold, *op. cit.*, and Beat, *op. cit.*

21. This surmise is supported by an occurrence in *Eliogabalo.* On f.69v

(II.9) an aria for Giuliano 'Io son più sfortunato' begins before the vocal entry and ends after the final statement by the voice. There are also three gaps between the vocal entries. On each of these five occasions, the word 'violini' appears in the score, in Cavalli's hand.

22. There is a similar occurrence in *Ipermestra* (I.9; f.22). Linceo's aria 'Caro bene' has been extended on to a separate sheet of paper, on the back of which is what appears to be a continuo part for a sacred piece. The page is marked 'tutti' at the top, although only a bass part is given. At each time change there are textual incipits, 'Vieni', 'Omnia' and 'Ideo', and at the foot of the page the direction 'Plaudite sopra l'altra carta'.

23. Sir Philip Skippon: *Journey through the Low Countries, Germany, Italy and France* (London, 1682; republished 1752), pp.520–1.

24. Performed at the Teatro San Cassiano; the librettist was Morselli.

25. *op. cit.*, p.521.

26. ASV, Scuola Grande di S Marco, b.188, f.279 and 269.

27. 'Tu vedi . . . un Drama composto per trattimento da una penna ch'è nobile, e rappresentato ne' Teatri frà lo spatio di vinti giorni; onde sei pregato di compatimento per la strettezza del Tempo . . .'

28. Performed at the Teatro S Moisè; music by Luccio.

29. 'Confesso anch'io riconoscerlo colmo d'imperfettioni. Tu lasciando da parte il satirizarlo, attribuisci il tutto alla fretta . . . perche dell'istesso tempo, che io componevo era posto alle note musicali . . .'

30. ASV, Scuola Grande di S Marco, b.194, f.116: a letter dated 13th December, 1665. '. . . riceverà tutto il reso del 2.0 Atto il 3.o Atto, et il Prologo, che vuol dire fornita tutta l'opera'. The opera concerned was *Alciade* (G. Faustini's libretto), which was not actually performed until 1667. The letter makes references to the roles of a Nocchiero and Serilda, both of whom appear in this opera.

31. For example: *ibid.*, b.194, f.138, a letter dated 20 December 1665. Cesti is referring to his opera *Tito*.

32. This surmise is based on the assumption that the performances opened on Boxing Day. There are clauses in singers' contracts obliging them to arrive in Venice by the middle of November. e.g. *ibid.*, b.194, f.110.

33. Performed at the Teatro SS. Giovanni e Paolo; music by Rovettino.

34. 'Per non fastidirti con la lunghezza del Drama, hò levato nell'ultime prove tutto quello, che hò stimato superfluo.'

35. Performed at the Teatro SS. Giovanni e Paolo; music by Sartorio.

36. 'Sappi di più, che per essere il Signor Clemente arrivato in tempo, ch'erano già dispensate li parti del Drama, m'è convenuto inserirlo nell'uno, e nell' altro al meglio, che hà potuto permettere la brevità del tempo; havendo havuto un solo riguardo, di non privarti del godimento della voce di un Virtuoso si insigne . . .' This singer could well be Signor

Clemente Hader, a renowned performer in his time, who was employed in Vienna from at least 1672 to 1687.

37. Performed at the Teatro S. Salvatore; music by Cesti.

38. *Ipermestra* (Cavalli–Moniglia) was performed in Florence in 1658.

39. This reference to an opera entitled *Fabio Massimo* is something of a mystery, for no evidence of its existence can be found in any of the normal sources. The recitative in the *Argia* prologue implies that either Draghi or Minato (who collaborated in *Ratto delle Sabine*) had a hand in it; for Apollo sings of both operas 'D'un istessa penna ambi son parti'. Fabio Massimo may possibly have been a prominent character in a historical opera of another name, perhaps Sbarra's *L'Amor della patria superiore ad ogn'altro* (Munich, 1665), or Noris's *Marcello in Siracusa* (Venice, SS. Giovanni e Paolo, 1670; music by Boretti).

40. *Ratto delle Sabine* (Draghi–Minato) was performed in Vienna in 1674 to celebrate the birthday of Emperor Leopold I. Although at first it seems highly unlikely that an aria from this opera was heard in Venice four years before its first full performance, Minato's preface reveals that the work had originally been written for Venice:

> 'Questo Drama fù concepito per le Scene dell'Adria, mà direttione d'Astri più fortunati l'hà scorto sù quelle di CESARE à festeggiare il Dì Natalizio del più insigne Monarca.'

41. *op. cit.* The contract states that Cavalli should be paid 400 ducats each year in the following manner: 150 ducats after the first performance, and 50 ducats after every subsequent five performances.

42. Bnm: Dramm.919.3.

43. *op. cit.*, p.516.

44. *Ibid.*, p.521.

45. *Prologue (spoken by Mr Garrick) At the Opening of the Theatre in Drury-Lane, 1747* (London, 1747).

CHAPTER IV

Sacred Music

It seems to have been customary for Venetian musicians holding prestigious positions at St Mark's to publish retrospective collections of their church music. Willaert published his *Musica Nova* in 1559; Andrea Gabrieli's *Concerti* were published posthumously in 1587; the first volume of Giovanni Gabrieli's *Sacrae Symphoniae* appeared in 1597, and the second was published posthumously in 1615 with his *Canzone e sonate*; Monteverdi's *Selva morale* of 1640 was followed after his death by his *Messa a 4 voci, et salmi* (edited by Cavalli) in 1650. Following the example of his illustrious predecessors, Cavalli similarly published two main volumes of sacred music, his *Musiche Sacre* in 1656, and the *Vespri* in 1675. These two publications, reinforced by a handful of individual works in various collections, and one manuscript, yield only 61 pieces. The figure is disappointingly low, particularly in view of the fact that Cavalli's output for St. Mark's must have been considerably more substantial. But the surviving pieces in the two large collections were clearly not produced simply for the printing presses, nor even necessarily at the time of publication. As had occurred when the sacred music of Willaert, the Gabrielis and Monteverdi was published, the collections were made at the instigation and encouragement of the publisher (Cavalli himself confirms this), and at crucial stages in his life. In 1656 his career was at its peak, in 1675 it was reaching its conclusion. An approximate appreciation of Cavalli's sacred compositions can therefore be pieced together and summarised, and his stature among his contemporaries can be duly assessed.[1]

The differences of style in Cavalli's church compositions,

ranging as they do from the large-scale to the small-scale, and from counterpoint to solo singing, are chiefly accounted for by non-musical factors. At the time of Cavalli's arrival in Venice, the Basilica's music was flourishing. Following Monteverdi's appointment as *maestro di cappella* three years earlier in 1613, the standard of performance had been gradually restored, and it was he who instituted the use of *prima prattica* counterpoint for ordinary services. From his earliest years there he began to collect a sturdy team of colleagues and subordinates upon whom he could depend and rely. The *vice-maestro de cappella,* M'A. Negri, was soon to be succeeded by Antonio Grandi in 1620, and later by Rovetta in 1630. With a musical team of such quality, St. Mark's was able to steer its way through the extreme problems presented by the plague of 1630, which considerably disrupted all musical activity. Standards were maintained, albeit with greatly diminished forces, and so the music that survives from these years is inevitably on a smaller scale. Towards the end of the 1630's a large number of appointments were made in a move to rebuild the musical staff to its full quota.[2] Gradually more large-scale works could be accommodated, and Cavalli's grandiose psalm-settings presumably date from the 1640's and 1650's. The works in his final publication are all for double choir and continuo only; they deploy the full choral forces available at St. Mark's, but reflect the slight weariness that is apparent also in his secular works from these years.

Considering Cavalli's output chronologically, the six pieces incorporated into casual publications before his major collection of 1656 may be taken together. (Those in *Musiche Sacre* must be examined as a unit for although many of them were written at the same time as those published earlier, the very fact that they were ultimately presented together implies an element of unity which was recognised by both composer and publisher.) The first six pieces are 'Cantate Domino'[3] in *Ghirlanda Sacra* of 1625, 'O quam suavis' in *Motetti a voce sola* of 1645, the Magnificat in Monteverdi's posthumously-published *Messa a 4 voci, et salmi* of 1650, and the three pieces 'In virtute tua', 'O bone Jesu' and 'Plaudite, cantate' published in *La Sacra Corona* in 1656. The first two are solo motets for single voice and continuo; both are essentially fluent, pleasing and unstartling. In accordance with the technique adopted in contemporary song-books (for example those of Grandi and Berti), a split between recitative and aria is gradually emerging. Both pieces are made up of comparatively short sections which alternate the two styles. Several characteristics of Cavalli's general style are also apparent. His technique of overlapping two sections by making the second anticipate its entry over the cadence of the first (a technique matched in his later operatic arias by string ritornellos beginning before the end of a vocal section) is evident in both pieces, and in 'Cantate Domino' there are also five-bar phrases, which foreshadow Cavalli's abandonment of standard four- and eight-bar lengths when a particular phrase (musical or textual) suggests itself to him. There are also extensions of phrase by word-repetition. Both pieces are in their home-key almost throughout; when Cavalli does venture into another key he often finds it difficult to return to his tonic. But 'O quam suavis' in particular is a neat little compendium of all the styles available to him, incorporating declamatory word-setting, triple-time quasi-arias with intermediary ritornellos, and elements of counterpoint with the voice and *basso continuo* in imitation. Although both pieces may be said to lack the maturity and variety of others in the same collections, they certainly merited their inclusion among works by more illustrious names (at that time) than Cavalli's own, and marked a competent debut into the competitive world of published music.

The Magnificat published in 1650 is scored for six voices (two sopranos, alto, two tenors and bass), two violins and continuo. In this first surviving large-scale work we can observe how Cavalli's naturally dramatic mind reacted to a comparatively lengthy text and produced a well-structured and neatly contrasted piece. The texture which emerges predominantly is that of the trio-sonata, for, of the sixteen individual sections, no fewer than eight either couple two voices with continuo, or feature the two violins with continuo, or even have three voices actually singing, but the lowest (tenor or bass) doubling the *basso continuo* line. Again the piece embraces all styles available to the composer; *stile antico* contrapuntal writing is contrasted with more modern harmonic word-setting, and with solo sections for one to three voices. A quasi-antiphonal effect, even in this comparatively small texture, is achieved in the 'Sicut locutus est' section by balancing two voices and continuo with two violins and continuo. There are occasional touches of more florid vocal writing in the solo sections, and in the large tuttis Cavalli creates a rhythmic impetus by having one inner part dislocated by one beat from the rest of the harmonic texture. All sixteen sections are smoothly dovetailed into each other, and so the overall result is fluent and balanced, with constant variety to maintain musical interest.

The three pieces published in Marcesso's 1656 collection, *La Sacra Corona,* are for two or three voices and continuo. Of these, the most interesting is clearly 'O bone Jesu', largely because of the quality of its text which could almost be described as an erotic poem. Set by Cavalli for soprano, alto and continuo, it is again a fluent and neatly joined piece, of little or no technical difficulty for singers. It is basically a syllabic setting throughout, with barely a trace of melisma, and only occasional suggestions of counterpoint to keep the impetus flowing and remove the danger of tedium. With the spontaneity of the true dramatic composer, Cavalli slips easily into different time-signatures ($\frac{3}{2}$ and $\frac{4}{2}$) according to the nuances of the text, as for example in the setting of the words 'Mea lux, meum cor, meum gaudium', where the rhythmic impetus gathers momentum through repetition and glides neatly into an appropriately triple-time extension of the word 'gaudium':

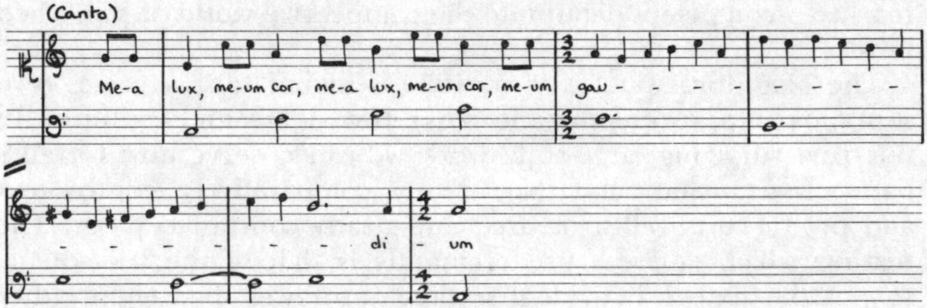

Rather in the manner of Monteverdi, Cavalli includes compelling false relations and dissonances at particularly passionate moments, and in true dramatic style creates a sudden stillness and calm at 'Respice mundi crimina'. (The effect of this unexpected immobility is not dissimilar to that created by Tallis in his mammoth 40-part setting of 'Spem in alium', also at the word 'Respice'):

But however much these first six pieces demonstrate a technical assurance, along with the fluent spontaneity that lends distinction to Cavalli's theatrical works, the complete span of his style in sacred composition is not fully encountered until the 1656 *Musiche Sacre* is examined. The collection comprises 28 pieces, ranging in style from the grandiose (double-choir psalms with concertato solo sections and a supporting instrumental band) to the intimate (hymns and antiphons for solo voice and continuo). There are eleven psalms, five hymns, four Marian antiphons, a complete Mass setting, a Magnificat and six instrumental canzonas in three to twelve parts; the whole collection is printed in twelve separate part-books. As Cavalli's preface states,[4] the main instruments are two violins and a violoncino. Three trombone parts are optional extras for five of the pieces, and printed into the alto, tenor and bass parts of the second choir.

Six pieces are in a large spectacular style, using two choirs, strings, continuo and trombones if desired. (By this time strings and trombones were the only instruments used in the Basilica; this reflects the move towards monochrome sounds and the departure from illustrative variations of texture.) The six are the Mass,[5] the Magnificat,[6] and four of the psalms; 'Dixit Dominus', 'Confitebor tibi Domine', 'Laudate Dominum'[7] and 'Lauda Jerusalem'. As is to be expected from such pieces when composed for St. Mark's, they depend largely on the textural contrasts of juxtaposing tutti sections with different solo combinations, balancing the two choirs antiphonally in the essentially Venetian polychoral traditions, and varying the vocal sounds occasionally with small ritornellos from the instruments alone. Within the solo sections (by now a permanent feature of sacred music) further variety is achieved by different combinations of voices, from one to four parts, and different styles, from regular counterpoint with its more obvious bar-lines and tonality, to monody with melisma and virtuoso elements. By means of these different combinations, musical variety is constantly achieved and the impetus duly maintained. The Mass setting perhaps demonstrates most clearly Cavalli's facility and technical competence with large-scale textures. It is likely that he wrote it in 1644 to celebrate the peace between the Pope and the Duke of Parma, whom Venice had supported, after four years of altercation.[8] Cavalli's conception of the work as a whole can only be described as dramatic, with its smooth juxtapositions and occasional sudden contrasts. Certain unmistakably secular tendencies creep in, such as the melodic use of the flattened third in the 'Crucifixus' section:

and even more strikingly in the setting of 'Et unam', a duet section for two solo altos. Here the vocal lines are melodically static and it is the bass line which moves and has the musical interest. Such a device is clearly reminiscent of operatic expressions of constancy, which Cavalli emphasised in precisely the same way:

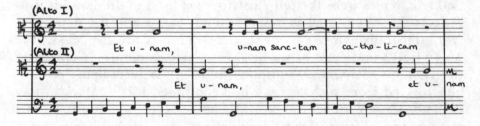

The 'Et incarnatus' further illustrates Cavalli's dramatic conception of the work. Immediately following an alto solo, 'Qui propter', built on a conventionally descending phrase for the word 'descendit', the 'Et incarnatus' uses the complete forces in solid block harmony, and creates a sensation of stillness, reverence and solemnity in the same way as the 'Respice' section of 'O bone Jesu'. In the tutti 'Gloria' the word 'pax' is deliberately delayed to create a quasi-dramatic effect, and as the impetus is picked up once more Cavalli immediately adopts his technique of removing a small portion of the text from its context and repeating it against the full statement of the line. Here it is the words 'in terra' which are so emphasised:

Cavalli makes economical use of material in this work. The 'Domine Deus' section of the 'Gloria' is set for alto, tenor and bass solos from the second choir; this leads to 'Domine fili' for other solo combinations using the same musical matter. Similarly the 'Qui tollis' and 'Qui sedes' sections of the same movement are based on identical material, although its execution is again varied by using different solo groups. The trio sonata texture is constantly employed, not just in the instrumental sections but also again in solo vocal sections where the lowest part (tenor or bass) may double the *basso continuo*. Refrain techniques are also used to integrate the various sections, as is Cavalli's practice also in the psalm settings.

Occasionally in these larger textures there are suggestions of technical insecurity on the part of the composer. In 'Laudate Dominum', for example, Cavalli only just manages to avoid forbidden consecutives between the second tenor and both the first alto and the second bass:

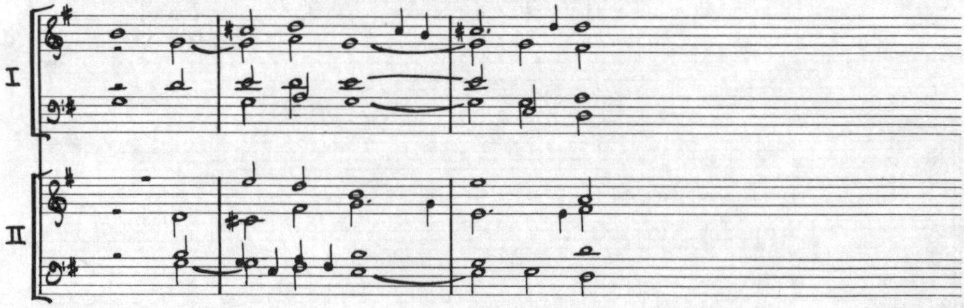

But elsewhere Cavalli atones admirably for such fleeting solecisms. In the same piece the doxology (which is musically longer than the complete setting of the main text) is superbly handled, with the musical and textual material delicately dispersed between various solo combinations, and contrasted with heavy tuttis where rhythmic activity in the inner parts ensures constant vitality. 'Lauda Jerusalem' similarly opens with a rousing and lively setting of the first line, which leads to a long solo section for individual voices separated by a recurring ritornello. This is itself followed by another large tutti section which, in all eight parts, uses the natural rhythms of the words to obtain vitality, particularly with the setting of:

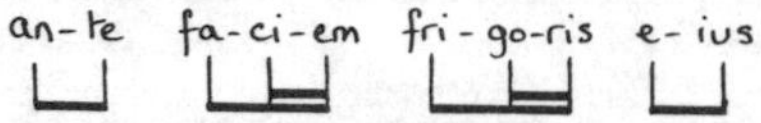

In the Magnificat, Cavalli's contrapuntal skills, even in large textures, are apparent at the setting of 'Esurientes', which is a comparatively extensive fugue in all parts on a lively subject:

These large-scale settings, then, show the composer to be thoroughly familiar with the building for which he was writing, and with the traditions that it had itself encouraged. At his best Cavalli continued to combine the spectacular element of the Basilica's performances with the intimacy often required by the texts that he handled.

The remaining seven psalms in the 1656 collection are on a less grandiose scale. 'Laudate pueri' and 'Credidi' are for a five-part choir (two sopranos, alto, tenor, bass) with strings and continuo; 'In convertendo' is for the same vocal forces and continuo, but without strings; 'Nisi Dominus' is for a four-part choir, strings and continuo; 'Beatus vir' and 'Laetatus sum'[9] for alto, tenor, bass, strings and continuo; and 'Domine probasti' for soprano, alto, bass, strings and continuo. It is in these pieces, which are not bound by the polychoral traditions of the larger settings or by the essentially repetitive structures of the smaller hymns and antiphons, that Cavalli's ties with the opera house are most apparent. 'Nisi Dominus' has several operatic touches. The words 'Sicut sagitte in manu potentis' towards the end of the main text are set for a bass solo. The length of this section (44 bars), its alternation between

$\frac{3}{2}$ and $\frac{6}{4}$ time, and particularly its employment of strings between all entries of the voice, combine to give it all the characteristics of an operatic aria. Earlier in the same work, the words 'Vanum est vobis ante lucem surgere' are set for a tenor solo alternating with an alto solo. The two singers share the text between them, and repeat it for musical extension, and their vocal entries are similarly relieved by string antiphons:

This section is again totally reminiscent of an operatic aria divided between two singers, or a horizontal duet. The feeling of the whole piece is in a similarly secular vein; there are captivating melismas on individual words such as 'doloris', with its diminished intervals, semitone clashes, unlikely leaps and flattened cadences:

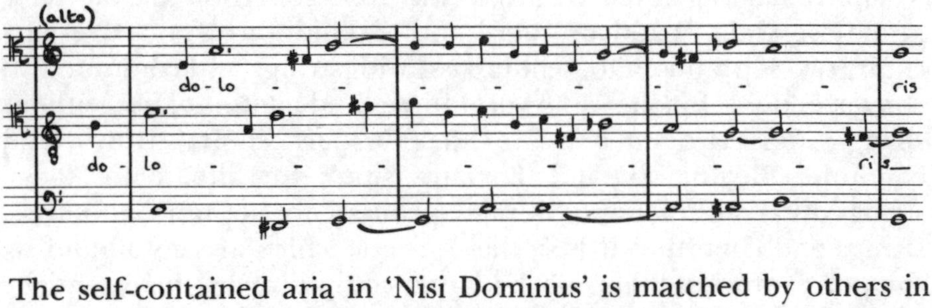

The self-contained aria in 'Nisi Dominus' is matched by others in this group of psalms. The setting of 'Laetatus sum' centres round a long solo section beginning with the words 'Illic enim ascenderunt'. The three singers (alto, tenor and bass) each sing out verse of the text; their entries are separated by a ritornello built on the opening phrase of the alto solo. In all cases the word-setting is straightforward, with occasional melismas on specially important words; and, because of the different ranges of voice, the vocal lines differ. But the bass line is identical for all three singers, and again one is reminded of the operatic strophic aria divided between three characters of different vocal ranges. 'Beatus vir' also incorporates a self-contained structure like an aria, at the alto solo's 'Paratum cor eius sperare in Domino'. In a similar number of bars to the bass solo in 'Nisi Dominus', it begins almost as recitative (with straightforward syllabic setting over a static bass) before moving smoothly into $\frac{3}{2}$ and alternating thereafter with $\frac{4}{4}$. The whole section is concluded by a ritornello, and again has the same fluency and spontaneity that characterises most of Cavalli's operatic arias.

Apart from such distinct operatic borrowings, these psalms continue to reveal Cavalli's own individual characteristics. 'Laetatus sum' contains an element of harmonic surprise with the setting of the words 'Fiat pax in virtute tua':

'Laudate pueri' has a flattened cadence at 'Sit benedictum':

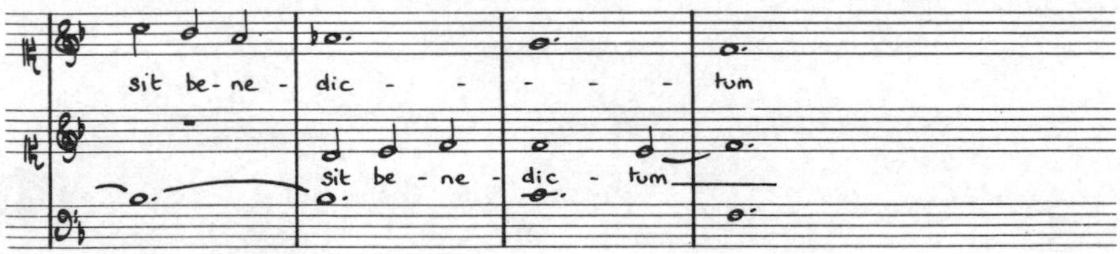

'Beatus vir' contains another instance of a static vocal line over a moving bass line because of the dictates of the text:

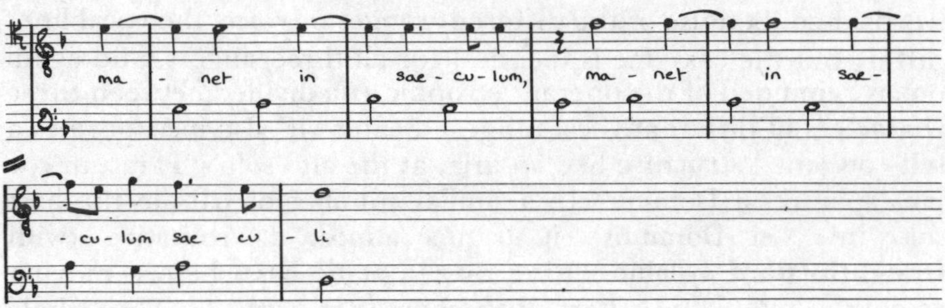

and 'In convertendo' is built almost entirely on a crotchet bass line. There are occasional hints that Cavalli was aware of settings of the same texts by his predecessors and contemporaries. In 'Beatus vir', for example, the word 'peribit' immediately before the doxology dies away in a manner not dissimilar to that of Monteverdi in his setting of the psalm, published in *Selva morale e spirituale* (1640):

(CAVALLI)

Quite apart from all these intriguing individual details, each psalm in this group is well constructed and carefully balanced. 'Laudate pueri' is possibly the most interesting, for it has an overall cumulative structure, beginning with thin solo textures (a bass solo leads to a duet between two sopranos and then to a trio for all three) which continue in various combinations until the last line before the doxology, 'Matrem filiorum laetantem', where all five voices come together for the first time. The doxology itself is again extensive, and comprises nearly half the total length of the piece. This psalm demonstrates Cavalli's technical competence at its most versatile. All five voices are of equal importance and have identical amounts of exposed solo singing; the tutti sections are well prepared and handled, and the strings are used for effective contrast in ritornello, only joining with the voices in the final 'Amen'. Such imaginative versatility distinguishes this group of psalms from the rest of the collection. At first sight they appear less interesting than the larger settings because of their smaller scale and relative simplicity; but they could arguably be described as the most characteristic of Cavalli, not merely in the 1656 collection, but also of the entire corpus of his surviving sacred compositions.

The five hymns are on a considerably smaller scale.[10] 'Exultet orbis' is for four voices, strings and continuo; 'Ave maris stella', 'Jesu corona virginum' and 'Deus tuorum militum' for alto, tenor, bass, strings and continuo; and 'Iste confessor' for two sopranos, strings and continuo. All are necessarily strophic and relatively simple, with instrumental ritornellos separating the strophes. 'Ave maris stella' is one of the most pleasing: of its seven strophes, the first and last are sung by the three singers together, and the intervening five are respectively given to alto, tenor, bass, tenor and bass. What becomes clear when the three voices join again for the final strophe is that their three solo lines are the same as those they sing in ensemble; that is, Cavalli has virtually composed the elements of a triple-subject contrapuntal piece, except that the material never has a chance to be expanded. It is an extension of the technique he adopted in the 'Illic enim ascenderunt' section of 'Laetatus sum'. The constant triple metre of this piece distinctly implies aria, and makes it perhaps one of the most telling indications of the composer's familiarity with the small-scale, self-contained solo structure. 'Iste confessor' likewise alternates between the two sopranos separately and together: they begin as a duet, the second strophe is for first soprano solo, the third strophe is the duet again, the fourth strophe is for the second soprano solo, and a final duet ends the hymn. 'Deus tuorum militum' deploys its three singers in a slightly different way. Each strophe has four lines, of which the first is sung by the tenor, the second by the alto, the third by the bass and the fourth by all three together, using delicately contrapuntal material. All lines are separated by string answers to the vocal statement, and the use of the crotchet bass line, particularly in its descending direction against the vocal phrases, is of elegant simplicity:

These hymns may be said to represent Cavalli's style in miniature, and as such are of considerable charm.

The four Marian antiphons[11] complete the vocal material in the collection. 'Alma redemptoris mater' is for two sopranos, alto, tenor, bass and continuo; 'Salve regina'[12] for alto, two tenors, bass and continuo; 'Regina coeli' for alto, tenor, bass and continuo; 'Ave regina coelorum' for tenor, bass and continuo. Of these, by far the most interesting is 'Salve regina', partly because of the quality of the text, which has inspired so many notable settings throughout the centuries. Once more Cavalli reveals his proficiency in many different styles, and his essentially dramatic approach to a text. Its *stile antico* opening soon gives way to a more broad, harmonic feeling at the words 'Vita dulcedo et spes nostra'. At the immediately ensuing 'Ad te clamamus' there is a sudden change of mood:

and at 'ad te suspiramus' the text is split up syllabically and separated by rests in a positively madrigalian manner:

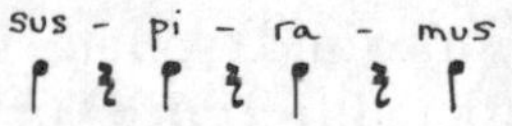

The section beginning 'Et Jesum benedictum fructum ventris tui' highlights another of Cavalli's old techniques, that of removing a word from its context and repeating it against the whole statement:

This too can only be described as dramatic. 'Regina coeli', with a slightly smaller texture, skilfully uses the three voices as soloists and in ensemble, in a way almost to suggest that there are more than three parts. The text-setting in 'Alma redemptoris mater' is somewhat unbalanced, for the last phrase takes up as much as three-quarters of the piece. This suggests that Cavalli composed his sacred music with the same spontaneity as he did his secular music, and allowed himself to be carried away musically only when the text permitted it. The vastly different lengths of psalm-settings in this collection bear out this surmise, as do the repeated occasions where the doxology constitutes a substantial proportion of the whole work.

Musiche Sacre finally contains six canzonas or sonatas, in 3, 4, 6, 8, 10 and 12 parts, continuing the practice of *sonata da chiesa.*[13] These were no doubt intended to be performed as voluntaries in church. The terms canzona and sonata were employed almost arbitrarily. There is little difference between the two types, although the four sonatas (the pieces in 4, 6, 8 and 12 parts) are perhaps in an older contrapuntal style, while the two canzonas (in 3 and 10 parts) are based on heavier canzona rhythms and style. Rather like their secular counterparts, sinfonia and ritornello, they had come to mean the same thing and were used interchangeably. The three largest pieces are predominantly homophonic and antiphonal, with relatively little melodic or contrapuntal interest, although the Sonata à 12 is quite a clever construction, opening with a double-subject fugue of which both subjects later reappear as harmonised melodies. But their chief interest was clearly in the spatial deployment of large sounds, and their effect in St. Mark's must have been spectacular. The smaller pieces were almost certainly written for establishments other than St. Mark's, following the traditions of Giovanni Gabrieli's Sonata à 3 (1610) for S Rocco. They are more obviously contrapuntal, relying heavily on the trio sonata texture. Again there are occasional examples of Cavalli's characteristic difficulty in avoiding consecutives when in more than three parts, as for example in the Sonata à 6:

But the most astonishing feature to emerge from these instrumental pieces is the final movement of the Canzona à 3. It is built entirely over twelve statements of an A minor descending tetrachord, with which Cavalli was so familiar in the opera house. Not only does this contrast vividly with the lively fugal movement which precedes it, but it also demonstrates without a doubt that Cavalli's creative muse was never far from his truly theatrical works. The 1656 *Musiche Sacre* constitutes not only the bulk of Cavalli's extant sacred music, but also its essence. Nowhere subsequently did he attempt to show such adventurous spirit in church pieces. The distinctly lament-type movement of this, the smallest piece in the collection, neatly summarises Cavalli's fidelity to his ecclesiastical duties, but also betrays his true inclinations.

As Cavalli himself had confessed in the preface to *Musiche Sacre,* he was reluctant to commit his music to print. Knowing this, it is perhaps not surprising, however much it is disappointing, to learn that his next major publication did not appear until the final months of his life. Three sets of Vespers, the *Vespero della Beata Vergine, Vespero delle Domeniche, e altre Salmi* and *Vespero delle Cinque Laudate,*[14] were published in Venice, by Gardano, in 1675. In the intervening years two of the motets from Marcesso's *Sacra Corona* of 1656 had been reprinted by Silvani in Bologna, in a collection entitled *Sacri Concerti* (1668), and Cavalli himself had of course been promoted to the illustrious post of *maestro di cappella* at St. Mark's in 1668. Yet, if the music of the 1675 publication is anything to go by, the administrative energy with which he approached his new job did not extend to keeping his own musical style abreast of current trends. Just as the style of his theatrical music had by now become obsolete, so his last sacred pieces rejected (or ignored) the exciting innovations of, for example, the Bologna school of composers,[15] and reverted completely to the antiphonal traditions of St. Mark's and occasionally to *stile antico* counterpoint. All the pieces in this final collection are scored simply for double choir and continuo. The psalms are competent, and slightly automatic. The quasi-secular departures from the old style that he himself had established in his earlier compositions are now abandoned. There are few remaining traces of the smooth section-overlaps which had lent so much fluency to his 1656 pieces: now the two choirs merely answer each other with a workmanlike predictability. He still achieves a certain degree of textural variety by alternating various solo combinations with the full forces, and in these solo sections the counterpoint is generally more elaborately sustained. But even here, the counterpoint is most successful only on relatively short subjects. When Cavalli has a long phrase to deal with, he cannot sustain or prolong it at all. This occurs at the point on 'Sicut locutus est' for the first choir in the Magnificat from *Vespero delle Domeniche:*

which soon lapses into slightly decorated homophony. The three Magnificats, one from each set of Vespers, continue to show these occasional signs of fatigue and automatic composition.[16] It is striking, for example, that all three employ the same harmonic change at the words 'Misericordia ejus' (C major to A major, thus juxtaposing C♮ and C♯). The Magnificat from the *Vespero della Beata Vergine* has two interesting features of its own. It opens, unusually, with a definite eight-part writing, as opposed to the habitual double-choir style of four against four:

But it soon proceeds to alternating the two choirs in the normal way. At the words 'Sicut locutus est' there is a brief reminder of Cavalli's old technique of removing words from their context and playing them against the complete statement of the text. The second choir echoes the first choir with the words 'Abrahae' and, later, 'et semine ejus', in a way that would make nonsense of the second choir's music were it not considered in the context of the first choir. But this is by now an unusual feature, and in the present setting certainly an isolated one.

Cavalli's final surviving sacred composition, and doubtless one of the last pieces that he ever wrote, is the *Missa pro defunctis*. He composed it, in a curiously morbid fashion, for his own funeral service. Like all the pieces in the 1675 collection, and following the traditions of previous Venetian settings of the Requiem (for example that of Croce in 1605), it is set in *stile antico* for double choir and continuo. But this work has none of the signs of fatigue that are so apparent in the Vespers: rather it exploits all the possibilities of the rich eight-part texture for which he is writing, and emerges as an astonishingly powerful piece. Its counterpoint is particularly emotional, deriving from the madrigalian style, and often incorporates harmonies that can only be described as startling. In this way the work can be seen as a precursor of the chromatic type of piece produced by Cavalli's Venetian successor Lotti (1667–1740) or by the later Neapolitan school of composers, headed by Leo (1694–1744). The reason why this work so conspicuously stands out from among its immediate contemporaries may well lie in the quality of the text. Like all Requiem masses, the work is centred round the noble medieval Latin poem 'Dies irae, dies illa', attributed to the thirteenth-century Franciscan Thomas of Celano. Written in trochaic, octosyllabic, monorhymed tercets, the poem has an enormously percussive strength which builds up insistently throughout its considerable length. It is not irrelevant to observe that the text has acquired several settings from all generations of composers, and that without a doubt the most outstanding came from essentially dramatic composers like Mozart, Verdi and Britten. If the drama inherent in the text inspired theatrically-minded composers to produce some of their best music, then Cavalli was no exception.

The Requiem is cast in seven main sections: the Introit (beginning 'Requiem aeternam, dona eis'), the Kyrie, the Sequence ('Dies Irae'), the Offertory (beginning 'Domine Jesu Christe, Rex gloriae!'), the Sanctus, Benedictus with Osanna, and the Agnus Dei. From a purely technical viewpoint, there is little apparent difference between this work and any of Cavalli's other pieces for double-choir and continuo. His usual habit of combining antiphonal singing, solo singing in various combinations, and *stile antico* counterpoint, still persist. A new departure, however, is the incorporation of plainsong incipits in two parts at the beginning of the Introit and the Agnus Dei, for example:

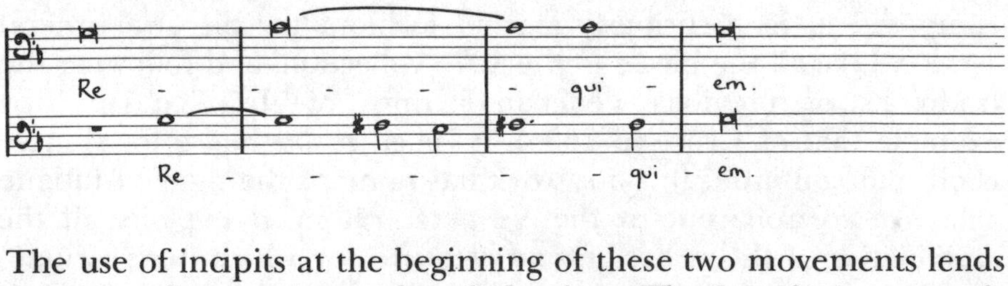

The use of incipits at the beginning of these two movements lends a degree of symmetry to the whole piece. The Introit soon reveals again Cavalli's technique of isolating a small section of text against the rest, when the word 'Exaudi' is emphasised by the second choir; meanwhile alto, tenor and bass solos from the first choir sing the whole line 'Exaudi orationem meam, ad te omnis carvo veniet'. Otherwise the Introit and Kyrie are of fairly standard quality, and it is not until the Sequence that the true power of Cavalli's work becomes apparent. The aggression of the opening line is immediately brought out in pounding repeated crotchets:

Apart from his rather surprisingly gentle setting of 'Tuba mirum' (for two sopranos and the first tenor), Cavalli constantly exploits the opportunities provided by the text for the contrasts that he so much valued. The three-part 'Tuba mirum' section is immediately followed by a solid eight-part harmonised setting of 'Mors stupebit', where the change of texture alone provides the electrifying effect that Cavalli sought. The section 'Judex ergo cum sedebit/Quidquid latet apparebit/Nil inultum remanebit' (When the judge sits, therefore, whatever now lies hidden will be exposed: nothing will remain unpunished) is set for soprano, alto and bass soloists from the second choir, and the word 'Nil' is isolated for dramatic emphasis:

Two stanzas later, 'Rex tremendae' is again set for the full eight-part choir, contrasting with the three-part texture of the previous stanza, and the poignant entreaty 'Salva me, fons pietatis', while still in eight parts, is a contrapuntal point beginning in one part only and gradually building up to all eight parts, stressing first the insecurity of the mere mortal and then the emotion behind his plea. Other dramatic devices and contrasts emerge later. The three-part 'Ingemisco tamquam reus' (I groan as a guilty one), set for low voices (alto, tenor and bass) and contrasting with the tessitura of the previous section scored for high voices (two sopranos and a tenor), colours the word 'ingemisco' with chromaticism:

'Confutatis maledictis' (when the accursed are confounded) is in a triple metre for the first time in the piece, but the confusion is emphasised by the use of cross-rhythms; immediately following this 'Voca me cum benedictis' (summon me along with the blessed) is back in sustained notes in , pleading and reverent. At the end of the 'Lacrymosa', the final prayer 'Pie Jesu Domine', possibly the climax of the whole poem, is defined by a broad setting with vivid harmonic juxtapositions:

The text of the Offertorium has a completely different character, and Cavalli communicates its inherent jubilation in a percussive syllabic setting. 'Quam olim Abrahae' goes into triple time again, thereby relieving with this movement the tension and emotion of its immediate predecessor. The 'Sanctus' provides further contrast: set in a solid eight-part texture virtually throughout, it incorporates mellifluous scale motifs used in sequence and in contrary motion. The breadth and relaxation of the setting achieve a level of sublimity not hitherto attainable in the text:

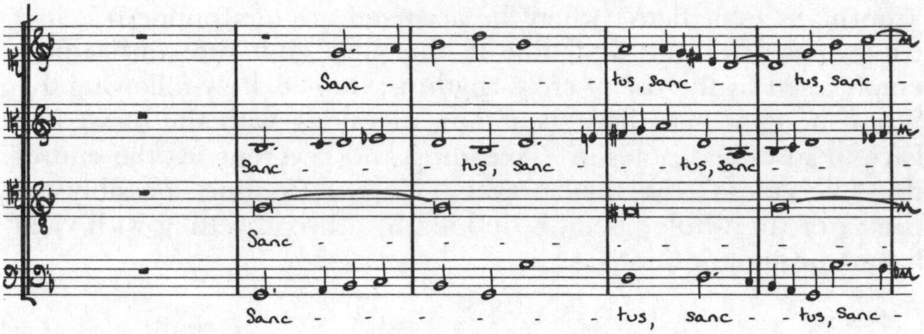

In the Osanna at the end of the 'Benedictus', the texture thickens and the tessitura rises. When the first soprano line touches a top F, the highest note in the whole work, its literally elevating effect is not dissimilar to that created by Monteverdi in the fourth act of *Orfeo* (1607). There Proserpina's plea to her husband on Orfeo's behalf gradually rose to an F, which shone through the sombre sounds deliberately used for the Underworld.

The work is still not without its minor technical insecurities: there are instances of parallel fifths or octaves (the 'Pie Jesu' above is one), and where Cavalli has spotted them himself he has attempted to remove them by some angular part-crossing (so that we do not see them, merely hear them). It seems that Cavalli never quite sorted out this problem. But the overall effect of this Requiem is nevertheless one of tremendous dramatic power and emotion. Its construction is symmetrical, with the broad outer movements framing the tension and activity in the central 'Dies irae'. Throughout, Cavalli has used dramatic contrast to the full, with constant juxtapositions of texture, harmony, tessitura, metre and musical style. He achieves further variety in the 'Dies irae' by setting the three-line stanzas to different lengths according to their content. In exactly the same way as he approached an opera libretto, he extends a phrase or word with spontaneity and dramatic fervour, thus totally avoiding the hazard of tedium (from the poem's regularity of metre and rhythm). Indeed, it is tempting to draw a parallel between Thomas of Celano's poem and Cavalli's setting of it. The poet's text transcended the potentially stifling restriction of its trochaic and octosyllabic form (which, as Longfellow demonstrated so admirably in *Hiawatha,* can easily sink into irritating monotony) and succeeded in producing what is generally known as the finest of all Medieval Latin poems. In the same way

Cavalli's composition transcended the stultifying limitations of its own conventions (double choir and continuo only, and the *stile antico* traditions) and resulted in a work that combined the most arresting drama with serene composure. Stylistically, therefore, this Requiem stands midway between Cavalli's two major sacred publications, for it combines the spontaneity of the early set with the maturity of his old age. As such, it was a not inappropriate conclusion to his life and to his musical composition.

To an extent, Cavalli's output of sacred music mirrors that of his secular composition. Its competent beginnings in the early pieces and smaller motets and psalms soon gave way to larger-scale works where he successfully combined spectacular effects with intimate expressions of reverence and humility. In the final years of his life his composition (with the exception of the Requiem) became somewhat stereotyped and lacked the fire and energy of his younger age. It is impossible not to draw further parallels between his secular and sacred music. The technical slips that crop up throughout the church pieces are present also in the operas: indeed, it seems that whenever Cavalli was writing in more than three parts, or not safely sheltered by the contrapuntal traditions of the *prima prattica* (lessons learned at a young age), he found himself in some trouble. On the other hand, one of his chief operatic assets, the ability to slot full arias fluently and almost unobtrusively into a coherent musical continuum, was also turned to use in his church music, for example at the bass aria in 'Nisi Dominus' and the two strophic arias in 'Laetatus sum' and 'Beatus vir'. Smaller sections $\frac{3}{2}$ similarly appeared throughout his pieces, as did the very secular features of chromatic word-painting, flattened cadences, and expressions of constancy (in 'Beatus vir' and the 1656 Mass). Occasionally the combination of secular and sacred styles is more clearly defined, as for example in 'Laetatus sum', where the 'Semper, semper' section of the doxology begins for an alto solo in triple time, but ultimately turns into a contrapuntal point between all three voices. A distinct feature of his sacred music, however, which passed into his secular works, was the use of strings as an antiphonal body. The interpolation of string 'answers' to vocal statements became the punctuating string interludes between the vocal entries of the operatic aria.

Generally Cavalli handled his individual pieces well, providing them with a neat, orderly structure. In 'Nisi Dominus', for example, the solo section beginning 'Cum dederit' is a succession of solo combinations, running tenor-bass, soprano-alto-tenor, alto-tenor and alto-tenor-bass; there is thus a symmetrical contour of tessitura. His solo sections are perhaps more interesting than his tutti sections. While he certainly could write large contrapuntal sections if necessary (for example the 'Esurientes' in the 1656 Magnificat), other polyphonic passages were often unsustained. What does emerge in an overall consideration of Cavalli's sacred music is a curious reversal in the church and in the opera house: the early sacred pieces are much more florid and vocally demanding than the later works, whereas in the opera house the situation was exactly the reverse. One reason is surely the fact that, just as Cavalli was an old man during his reign as *maestro di cappella,* so were many of his singers. Among them, for example, was Monteverdi's eldest son Francesco, who had been appointed to the choir in 1623. When Legrenzi became *maestro di cappella* in 1685 he set about reshuffling the choir and injecting some younger talent into it, rather as Monteverdi himself had done seventy years earlier. It follows that the type of music written by an old man for old singers was likely to be retrospective. A contributing element in this situation was of course the fact that opera had gradually become the most important art-form for composers and singers alike, and as they increasingly concentrated upon it, so their attention to sacred music waned. With Cavalli himself this had undoubtedly been so. All his life he served St. Mark's and he supplied it constantlywith the kind of music that it demanded, some of an exceptional quality. But the outstanding moments were those which were the most secular in style and feeling. Consequently, assuming his extant sacred works to be truly representative of his sacred output as a whole, it may be concluded that Cavalli's preference for the opera house did not affect the quantity of his pieces for the church, but perhaps betrayed itself in the quality.

NOTES

1. For previous considerations of Cavalli's sacred music, see: F. Bussi: 'La produzione sacra di Cavalli e i suoi rapporti con quella di Monteverdi' in *RIM* II, I (1967), pp.229–254. D. Arnold: 'Cavalli at St Mark's' in *Early*

Music IV,3 (1976), pp.266–274. For a complete list of extant works, see Appendix II.

2. For a list of these appointments, see E. Selfridge-Field: *Venetian Instrumental Music* (Oxford, 1975), Appendix F, pp.297–308.

3. ed. F. Vatielli in *Antichi cantate spirituali* (Turin, 1922)

4. See Appendix III⅞v.

5. ed, R. Leppard (London, 1966).

6. ed. R. Leppard (London, 1973).

7. ed. R. Leppard (London, 1969).

8. Fustinioni's revision of Francesco Sansovino's *Venetia città nobilissima* (*op. cit.*) states that on May 1st, 1644 'fù in Venetia publicata la Pace trà il Pontefice, Duca di Parma, e Collegati in chiesa di San Marco, dove fù cantata una Messa solenne pro Gratiarum actione'. (*Cronico Veneto*, p.72).

9. ed. R. Leppard (London, 1969).

10. For a consideration of this type of hymn, see: D. Arnold: 'A background note on Monteverdi's hymn settings' in *Scritti in onore di Luigi Ronga* (Milan–Naples, 1973).

11. All four Marian antiphons have been edited by B. Stäblein in *Musica Divina* i-iv (Regensburg, 1950).

12. Also ed. R. Leppard (London, 1969).

13. See S. Bonta: 'The Uses of the Sonata da Chiesa' in *JAMS* XXII,1 (1969), pp.54–84.

14. The *Vespero delle Cinque Laudate* presumably refers to specific ceremonies, whose meaning is not now clear, in St Mark's.

15. For contemporary church music in Bologna, see: A. Schnoebelen: 'Performance practices at San Petronio in the Baroque' in *AM* XLI (1969), pp.37–55.

16. All three have been edited, and elaborated, by G. Picciolo (Milan, 1960).

CHAPTER V

Reputation and Influence

The surviving documentary material relating to Cavalli's affairs, both professional and private, does occasionally yield certain fragments of information about his personality. Piecing these together, it is possible to assemble some sort of picture of the man's character. His was a generous, honest and probably very sympathetic nature. From his earliest years in Venice he always had the loyal support of various friends to whom he could turn if in trouble, from Federico Cavalli and his family, to Volpe, Minato, Marco Faustini and Claudio Paulini. His care for his wife and her family lasted for the whole of his life, and in his final will he distributed his considerable estate with care and benevolence. Yet running alongside this warmth of character was an able and lucid mind with an infinite capacity for clear thinking and administration. He managed his own career judiciously (he seemed to have the knack of working for the right theatres at the right time), and with similar practicality he supervised his inherited properties and the investing of the profits that they yielded. On the smaller scale he issued perspicuous directions to performers, both in his 1656 *Musiche Sacre* publication and in his score of *Ercole Amante* for Paris. As far as we can tell from the few surviving documents, his own accounts and his organisation of papers were neat and orderly. Against this almost hard clarity of mind, there was perhaps a thread of isolation and vulnerability. It is likely that it stemmed from his early wrench from his family as far back as 1616, but it manifested itself in the depression brought about by his French experiences, and his almost defeatist attitude towards the composing of operas thereafter. But the picture that builds up is one of a comfortably prosperous man, who combined the ability to be tough with the ability to be humane; he was probably an extremely likeable man to know.

Documentary evidence, then, reveals something of the man and his character; the pity is that more does not survive. There are considerable gaps and losses, particularly for example in comparison with Monteverdi, whose many surviving letters throw so much additional light on his personality. As with many other composers, we are reduced to a measure of speculation. But the principal source of evidence of Cavalli's character is his music. It has already been shown that he composed with spontaneity and fluency, and his immediate reaction to his texts revealed sensitivity, wit and understanding. He always obeyed the effect, as Handel did, and as Bach did not. The occasional flash of artistic temperament shown in his letters is confirmed also in his scores. His greatest successes were in his handling of the most extreme emotions: passion (with rapturous love duets), desolation (with tragic laments and intensely chromatic recitative), fury (in turbulent and aggressive outbursts) and insanity (wild arioso passages with ungainly leaps and bizarre dissonances). He also had a flair for comedy, and he excelled in lively burlesque. And yet the isolation and vulnerability is also present, for there seems to be a certain professional detachment between himself and his music. Surveying his output as a whole, it is impossible to detect in his compositions the difficult periods of his life, with the sole exception, perhaps, of the French incident. But in the works of either Monteverdi or Mozart there was an almost autobiographical element which penetrated whatever form the music took and allowed the listener or reader to be aware of personal elations and depressions. This was not so with Cavalli, nor even with Haydn. Their music admirably supplied all that was required of it, and often a great deal more; but it never gave anything away.

Cavalli's reputation was considerable both at home and abroad. The invitations from Milan, Florence, Paris and Piacenza speak for themselves, while in Venice itself certain published acknowledgements of his talents established his position in musical life. As early as 1642, Fusconi's preface to *Amore innamorato,* performed at the Teatro S moisè, stated:[1]

All the imperfections (of the libretto) however, are compensated

> by the gentleness of the music of Signor Francesco Cavalli, who has rightly become known as the Amphion of our time.

Similar tributes are to be found in *Ciro* (1654) and *Statira* (1656). But Cavalli's renown was not limited to opera, for he was equally acclaimed as a singer and an organist. In 1647 the German Paul Hainlen regretted that 'Sig. Gaballi' was heard too little, for he was the greatest organist at St. Mark's and comparable to Frescobaldi.[2] In 1671 Nicolo Doglioni's *Le cose notabile et maravigliose della città di Venezia* (originally published in 1596) was revised. Describing the musicians at St. Mark's, E.G. Zittio said:[3]

> Truly Francesco Cavalli has no equal in Italy, either in his exquisite singing, or in his noble organ-playing.

Even during his French visit, Cavalli met with some genuine admiration which was publicly acknowledged. The organist François Roberday wrote a fugue on a subject taken from Cavalli, and in the preface to its publication, in *Fugues, et caprices* (Paris, 1660), he declared that Cavalli's arrival in France, in the service of the King, had coincided with his publication, and that just in time he had begged him for a subject.[4] Finally in 1681 the dramatist Cristoforo Ivanovich (among those librettos had been *Coriolano* for Cavalli in 1669) compiled a chronological table of operas performed in Venice, in a collection of essays entitled *Minerva al Tavolino*. Published under the heading *Memorie teatrale*, the list was, as the title implies, based almost entirely on memory. Whenever he failed to remember the exact details of an opera's composer, Ivanovich tended to state that it was by Cavalli, with the result that until very recently a number of works have been wrongly attributed to him.[5] This publication has caused some havoc in musicological circles, but it cannot be denied that Ivanovich's casual attribution to Cavalli of any opera whose composer he could not accurately remember, is a fair indication of Cavalli's stature in operatic composition.

Having assessed Cavalli's position in his own time, the task of considering him in the context of musical history as a whole becomes more difficult. After his death there was little immediate continuation of his music, partly because he had had a few disciples, and of these none was of particular note. His Venetian pupils had included his friends Caliari and Volpe, as well as the two nuns of S Lorenzo, Francesca Grimani and Betta Mocenigo, to whom he had bequeathed certain items in his will. None of these was of any consequence. His most distinguished pupil was Barbara Strozzi. The adopted daughter of the poet Giulio Strozzi, she was a remarkable woman, a member of the Accademia degli Incogniti, and, with the Florentine Francesca Caccini (the daughter of Giulio Caccini), one of the earliest acclaimed female composers. In the preface to her second publication, a collection of cantatas and arias for one, two and three voices (1651), she acknowledged her debt to Cavalli, stating that he was one of the most outstanding men of the century, and that he had taught her since her childhood.[6] But she too was ultimately of little importance. Cavalli's musical legacy was not therefore immediate, since there was no composer or group of composers who acted instantly on the developments that he had made (as was to be the case, for example, with Haydn and Mozart in the following century). Again it is the shape of his career which accounts for this. At his peak Cavalli virtually reigned supreme in his own field, and his techniques were imitated by his contemporaries. But by the time of his death the new developments were being made away from his achievements and not directly as a result of them.

Certain of Cavalli's individual traits can be seen to have passed into the works of other nations. He and his Italian contemporaries were after all crucial to foreign composers who made the European Grand Tour and assimilated various styles and techniques. He himself was visited by J.P. Krieger in 1672, and possibly also by J.W. Franck.[7] His operas in France probably influenced Lully more than the latter would admit, both in the fluidity of melody and in the handling of the orchestra. There was also an oblique influence in England, where the Restoration composers were more than ever continuing their awareness of transalpine music. The diaries and travel accounts of such Englishmen as John Evelyn and Sir Philip Skippon conveyed their enthusiasm for contemporary Italian opera, and Evelyn reported, on 5 July 1674, that he had seen 'an Italian opera in music, and first that had been seen in England of this kind'.[8] A copy of Cavalli's own *Erismena* reached Britain at some stage in the seventeenth century, when it was translated into English.[9] It remained in sufficiently wide circulation in the following century for Burney to be familiar with it, and to include arias from it in his *General History of Music* (1789).[10] From these exiguous pointers, it might be speculated that Purcell had some knowledge of Cavalli's music. Certainly some of the music in *Dido and Aeneas* suggests that he was a musical heir to Cavalli: the general chromaticism, the tragic intensity and the overall dramatic impetus of the piece are all close parallels with Cavalli's own operas. Above all it is the final lament for Dido, 'When I am laid in earth', which bears the most striking resemblance. It is built, as were the majority of Cavalli's laments, on a descending , chromatic ground bass, whose shape is almost identical to that for the aria 'Piangete occhi' in Cavalli's *Egisto* of 1642 (II.6):

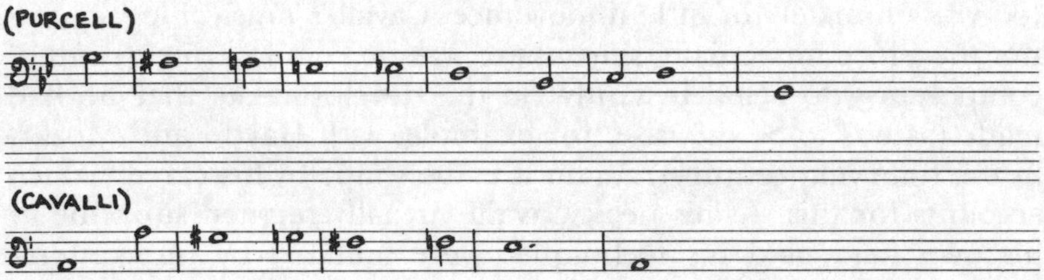

But Lully and Purcell too were responsible for the kind of composition that reached a peak with them and then ceased. The French brand of opera that Lully eventually produced was a solitary achievement, based as it was on the single-minded and even egocentric principles that he chose to adopt. After his death in 1687, French opera audiences had to wait until 1733 for the 50-year-old Rameau to formulate a style of composition that made positive developments in a specifically French style. Similarly in England, the self-conscious attempts of the Restoration composers to produce their own dramas in music resulted in only two immortal freaks, Blow's *Venus and Adonis* and Purcell's *Dido and Aeneas,* and otherwise a plethora of competent incidental music. It was not until the Italian companies arrived in London during the first decade of the eighteenth century that operatic tastes in England were properly awakened.

Neither the sacred nor the secular compositions of Cavalli can therefore be said to have had a lasting effect on the unfolding history of music. But the operas at least can be seen as representing the first large-scale peak in the history of the form. From the principles of the Florentine composers at the turn of the seventeenth century, the operatic aim was constantly to combine drama with music, add the dimension of spectacular staging, and to produce an art-form whose total exceeded the sum of its component parts. Throughout the course of operatic history one of these essential ingredients has from time to time been over-emphasised at the expense of the others, but the chief operatic reformers, such as Gluck and Wagner, have regularly reverted to the basic ideal. In considering the relevance of Cavalli's operas, then, it cannot be denied that his career was well timed. From this point of view his unfortunate successor and compatriot Alessandro Scarlatti can be said to have been born at the wrong time operatically, for he had to condition his considerable dramatic talents to what had become an essentially non-dramatic convention. Cavalli, on the other hand, was indisputably born at the right time, and the peak of his career coincided with that of seventeenth-century Venetian opera as a whole

In creating any opera which is to succeed and survive as theatrical entertainment, certain essentials must be sought. First, there should be a lively, original, coherent and well-structured story, with contrasts between serious and comic characters, variety of pace and mood, and preferably a satisfactory outcome and conclusion. Further it should supply variety in its settings, providing visual contrast and allowing all parts of the acting area, including the air, to be used. The musical score should then permit this story to proceed fluently. It should sustain, and indeed enhance, its more static moments by means of memorable and affective tunes, and to the contrasts already provided in the text add those of texture. Above all, there should be an overall malleability in the combination of text and score, with no unintentional abrupt juxtapositions, but with the confines of aria and recitative moulded to fit whatever the dramatic moment demands.

Cavalli's operas, and particularly those of the 1650's, provided the most balanced combination of these essential ingredients in seventeenth-century Italy. As true representatives of their period, their own contribution may now be summarised and considered in the general evolution of the form. The first, and most important, advance was the delineation of the aria. We have seen that during the course of the decade closed forms became more numerous and more clearly defined. In the long term this development was to prove disadvantageous, for it led to the break-down of dramatic fluency as arias became all-important; but during these early stages the contrasts of pace that it yielded were distinctly beneficial. Secondly, the historical plot was reintroduced in the 1650's. Such works as Minato's *Xerse* or *Antioco* established a new type of libretto, which was soon preferred to the freely-invented narratives of Faustini's time, and was retained almost continuously for the rest of the century. Thirdly, these operas had discovered the right level of complexity that a libretto could reasonably convey. The line of complicated intrigue had been developed to almost unmanageable proportions in *Eritrea, Statira* and *Erismena,* but by *Antioco* it had been tempered to a more realistic level. This too was retained in the 1660's: the plots of, for example, *Scipione Affricano, Muzio Scevola* and *Pompeo Magno* are historically-based, but the motivations of their chief characters are twisted and refocussed in order to accommodate the right amount (but not too much) of complicated intrigue. Finally, these operas may also be said to have established the comic servant characters, the sub-plots between them and the nature of their relationships with their masters. A new dramatic balance between comic and serious roles was introduced by the younger generation of librettists, resulting in the completely different structures of (for example) *Oristeo* and *Erismena.*

Four particular features, then, of Cavalli's operas were all assimilated into the general development of the form. But other developments made during these years were ultimately rejected. Of these, the first was the narrowing of forces and textures. This was practised chiefly by Cavalli and Giovanni Faustini at the Teatro Sant' Apollinare, whose confines presented them with little alternative. Nonetheless the prominence of these men resulted in this trend becoming fashionable, and composers and authors copied them even in theatres where it was by no means necessary. The size of Sant' Apollinare was not the only cause, for there were other factors of a political and economic nature. But it is unquestionable that when Sant' Apollinare ceased to be a profitable concern and the influential men moved to the larger theatres on a more permanent basis, the forces and textures expanded accordingly.

In the musico-dramatic structure, the most significant rejection that occurred after Cavalli's return from France was that of recitative for powerful expression. Throughout the 1640's and 1650's Cavalli in particular had used both aria and recitative almost interchangeably at moments of intense passion and feeling, and his ability to do so accounts for the tremendous energy, spontaneity and variety that his scores of this period possess. None of his contemporaries equalled him in this respect. Cesti and Ziani, for example, seemed always to be aiming at the aria text, which provided the opportunity for the good tune. Taking their operas and those of Cavalli aria by aria, it is probably true that they wrote more consistently fine individual numbers than he did. But with their scores it is almost possible to become bored by successions of good tunes when the intervening recitative material is of a lesser quality. It is the continuity in Cavalli's scores, through the parity betwen aria-quality and recitative-quality, which distinguishes his music from that of his fellows. Once the aria began to dominate, the balance was distorted. Recitative was relegated to a position of a mere link between closed forms; the significance of the drama itself was reduced and the whole operatic focus shifted. This transformed dramatic pattern laid solid foundations for the type of structure that persisted for almost a century. The inexorable succession of *da capo* arias linked by recitative proved a convention that could only be profitably exploited by a composer of the stature of Handle, who achieved operatic immortality through the drama inherent in his music. While there is no doubt that the works of the 1660's and later decades continued to provide individual arias of outstanding beauty and merit, they were never able to sustain the dramatic equilibrium and fluency that Cavalli's operas from the 1650's had provided. Cavalli's successors were primarily composing for the singers, but he himself wrote for the librettist and for the audience, recounting the story in music (truly *dramma in musica*) in the most natural way.

In the context of the general history of music, then, Cavalli was a vitally important figure. He learned from Monteverdi, and at his peak had a strong influence on other composers, both in and out of Venice. His solid talent stabilised the form for the benefit of later composers, and at the same time he produced some unquestionably immortal works, which have been revived today with great success. It is perhaps true to say that Cavalli was to Monteverdi as Handel was to Bach. His talents were for the overall effect and the instant result, and they were applied with largesse. There is absolutely no inner intricacy, as the constant consecutives show. His scores give the impression that he rarely took trouble over his compositions beyond the initial outpouring: that he simply trusted his own spontaneity. There were perhaps one or two revisions of individual passages, but he did not slave laboriously over meticulous detail; and it is likely that the final result would have been no better if he had.

But however much we may evaluate the parts of an opera by dissection and scrutiny, it is ultimately in the theatre that the work as a whole succeeds or fails. The seventeenth-century librettists themselves, whose printed texts were available to the public without their musical and theatrical contexts, were often anxious to stress this point. Aureli concluded his preface to *Perseo* (1665) with the plea:[11]

> Do not judge this work by its shadow on the printed page, until you have seen it in the theatre.

The ultimate testimony of an opera's worth, then, must surely come from the audiences. The final word is therefore taken from the English traveller Robert Bargrave, who concluded a seven-year Grand Tour of Europe with a visit to Venice in the Carnival season of 1655. His enthusiasm was boundless:[12]

> The Varieties of Carneval enterteinments are as unconfin'd, as are mens Fancies, Every minute and every place affording new. But above all, surpassing whatsoever theyr Inventions can else stretch to, are theyr Opera's (or Playes) represented in rare Musick from the beginning to the end, by select Eunuchs and women, sought out through all Italy on purpose.

He went on to conclude that the operas he witnessed (which almost certainly included at least one by Cavalli) had given him much more pleasure than had all his previous European experiences:[13]

> Nay I must needs confess that all the pleasant things I have yet heard or seen, are inexpressibly short of the delight I had in seeing this Venetian Opera; and as Venice in many things surpasses all places else where I have been, so are these operas the most excellent of all its glorious Vanities.

NOTES

1. 'A tutte l'imperfettioni però supplirà le soavità della Musica del Signor Francesco Cavalli, che con ragione vien creduto l'Anfione de' nostri giorni . . .' (Amphion, one of the twin sons of Antiope and Zeus, built the city of Thebes by playing on his harp with such skill that the stones were drawn into place by his music.)
2. Letter of 1 November 1647. See Bianconi: 'Caletti', *op. cit.*, p.686.
3. 'Francesco Cavalli veramente in Italia non hà pari, et per esquisitezza del suo canto, et per valore del suono dell'organo'. (Zittio was a pseudonym for Ziotti.)
4. . . . (Cavalli) estant venu en France pour la service du Roys, lors que mon Livre s'achevoit d'imprimer, je l'ay prié de me donner un sujet.'
5. See Walker: 'Gli errori di *Minerva al tavolino*', *op. cit.*
6. '. . . Signor Francesco Cavalli, uno de' più celebri di questo secolo, già dalla mia fanciullezza mio cortese precettore . . .'
7. See Walker: 'Cavalli' in *Grove* 6 (forthcoming).
8. John Evelyn: *Diary* (first published 1818; ed. E.S. de Beer, Oxford, 1955).
9. Now owned by Mr J. Stevens Cox, Guernsey.
10. Charles Burney: *A General History of Music* (London 1789), III, pp.63–5.
11. Performed at the Teatro SS. Giovanni e Paolo; music by Mattioli.
12. Account of a Grand Tour, 1648–1655. Oxford, Bodleian Library: MS Rawlinson C.799, ff. 173–4.
13. *Ibid.*

APPENDIX I

1. *The operas of Cavalli*

DATE	TITLE	LIBRETTIST	THEATRE	SCORE	ADDITIONAL COMMENTS
1639	*Le Nozze di Teti e di Peleo*	Persiani	S. Cassiano	Vnm	
1640	*Gli Amori di Apollo e di Dafne*	Busenello	S. Cassiano	Vnm	
1641	*La Didone*	Busenello	S. Cassiano	Vnm	
1642	*L'Amore innamorato*	Fusconi	S. Moisè	LOST	Fusconi revised the libretto from a plot by Loredano and poetry by Michiele
1642	*La Virtù de' strali d'Amore*	Faustini	S. Cassiano	Vnm	
1643	*L'Egisto*	Faustini	S. Cassiano	Vnm	Additional score in A–Wn
1644	*L'Ormindo*	Faustini	S. Cassiano	Vnm	
1645	*La Doriclea*	Faustini	S. Cassiano	Vnm	
1645	*Il Titone*	Faustini	S. Cassiano	LOST	
1649	*Il Giasone*	Cicognini	S. Cassiano	Vnm	Additional scores in A–Wn, B–Bc (2 modern copies), I–Fn, MOe, Nc, Rvat, Sc, P–La, GB–Ouf. Part of it was edited by R. Eitner in *PAMw* (1883)
1649	*L'Euripo*	Faustini	S. Moisè	LOST	
1650	*L'Orimonte*	Minato	S. Cassiano	Vnm	
1651	*L'Oristeo*	Faustini	Sant'Apollinare	Vnm	
1651	*La Rosinda*	Faustini	Sant'Apollinare	Vnm	
1652	*La Calisto*	Faustini	Sant'Apollinare	Vnm	
1652	*L'Eritrea*	Faustini	Sant'Apollinare	Vnm	
1653	*La Veremonda*	Strozzi	SS. Giovanni & Paolo	Vnm	Strozzi (under the pseudonym L. Zorzisto) revised the libretto from Cicognini's *Celio*

					(Florence, 1646). *Veremonda* was performed in Naples in December, 1652, before being transferred to Venice.
1653	*L'Orione*	Melosio	MILAN	Vnm	Additional score in the private collection of Raymond Leppard
1654	*Il Ciro*	Sorrentino	SS.G & P	Vnm	Originally performed in Naples (music by F. Provenzale). Cavalli added the prologue and some arias for Venice. Additional score in MOe.
1654	*L'Ipermestra*	Moniglia	FLORENCE	Vnm	Not performed until 1658
1655	*Il Xerse*	Minato	SS.G & P	Vnm	Additional score in Pn, I-Rvat.
1656	*La Statira*	Busenello	SS.G & P	Vnm	Additional score in I–Mc.
1656	*L'Erismena*	Aureli	Sant'Apollinare	Vnm	There are two scores in Vnm, one dating from the 1656 production and the other from a later revival. An additional score was in the private collection of T. Bever in the 18th century. A further score, with anonymous English translation, is now in the collection of J. Stevens Cox, Guernsey.
1657	*L'Artemisia*	Minato	SS.G & P	Vnm	
1659	*L'Antioco*	Minato	S. Cassiano	LOST	
1660	L'Elena? (in Berk. cat.)	Faustini–Minato	S. Gassiano	Vnm	
1662	*Ercole Amante*	Buti	PARIS	Vnm	
1664	*Scipione Affricano*	Minato	SS.G & P	Vnm	Additional scores are in I–Rvat, Sc, and P–La (Act III only)
1665	*Muzio Scevola*	Minato	S.Salvatore	Vnm	
1666	*Pompeo Magno*	Minato	S.Salvatore	Vnm	An additional score is in D–AN.
1668	*Eliogabalo*	Aureli	—	Vnm	Aureli completed the libretto, originally the work of another (anonymous) writer.
1669	*Coriolano*	Ivanovich	PIACENZA	LOST	
1673	*Massenzio*	Bussani	—	LOST	

APPENDIX I (continued)

2. *Doubtful operas:* those formerly attributed to Cavalli. In all cases the music is lost.

1642	*Narciso ed Ecco immortali* (in fact by Marazzoli and Vitali)	Persiani	SS. G & P
1644	*Deidamia*	Herrico	T. Novissimo
1645	*Il Romolo e il Remo* (possibly by Barbara Strozzi)	Strozzi	SS. G & P
1646	*La prosperità di Giulio Cesare dittatore*	Busenello	SS. G & P
1648	*La Torilda*	Bissari	SS G & P
1650	*Il Bradamante*	Bissari	SS. G & P
1651	*L'Armidoro* (possibly by G. Sartorio)	B. Castoreo	S. Cassiano
1653	*Helena rapita da Teseo*	Badoaro	SS G & P
1660	*La pazzica al trono* (not an opera at all)	Gisberti	Sant'Apollinare

3. *Revivals of operas* (with date of original performance given first)

1640	*Gli Amori di Apollo e di Dafne*	1647	Bologna
1641	*Didone*	1650	Naples
		1652	Genoa
		1655	Piacenza
		?1660	Milan
1642	*La Virtù de' strali d'Amore*	1648	Bologna
1642	*Egisto*	1645	Genoa
		1646	Florence
		1647	Bologna
		1648	Ferrara
		1651	Naples
		1659	Bologna
			Bergamo
		1661	Palermo
		1667	Florence
			Modena
1649	*Giasone*	1649	Milan
		1650	Lucca
			Florence
			Milan?
		1651	Naples
			Bologna
		1652	Florence
		1655	Piacenza
		1656	Leghorn

		1658	Vicenza
		1659	Ferrara
			Viterbo
		1660	Milan
			Valletri
		1661	Genoa
			Naples
		1663	Perugia
		1665	Ancona
			Viterbo
		1667	Brescia?
			Naples
		1668	Reggio Emilia
		1671	Rome (adapted by Stradella)
		1672	Naples
		1673	Bologna
		1676	Rome
		1681	Genoa
	(titled *Il trionfo d'Amor delle vendette*)	1685	Genoa
	(titled *Medea in Colco*)	1690	Brescia
1651	*Oristeo*	1653	Genoa
	(titled *L'Oristeo travestito*)	1656	Bologna
1651	*Rosinda* (titled *Le Magie amorose*)	1653	Naples
1653	*Eritrea*	1654	Bologna
	(titled *Vicendo d'Amore, overo Eritrea*)	1655	Genoa
		1659	Naples
		1661	Venice (T. S. Salvatore)
		1665	Brescia
1654	*Ciro*	1654	Genoa
		1657	Palermo
		1660	Leghorn
		1666	Bologna
		1671	Bologna
		1675	Modena
		1678	Perugia
1654	*Ipermestra*	1669	Genoa?
		1680	Pisa
1655	*Xerse*	1656	Genoa
		1657	Naples
			Bologna
		1658	Palermo

		1665	Milan
			Verona
		1667	Turin
		1682	Cortona
1656	*Statira*	1665	Bologna
		1666	Naples
1656	*Erismena*	?1656	Bologna
		1661	Bologna
			Milan
			Florence
		1662	Ferrara
		1666	Brescia
			Genoa
			Ancona
		1668	Bologna
			Lucca
		1669	Ferrara
		1670	Venice (T. S. Salvatore).
		1673	Forli
1657	*Artemisia*	1658	Naples
		1659	Palermo
		1662	Milan
		1663	Milan
		1665	Genoa
1660	*Elena*	1661	Palermo
1664	*Scipione Affricano*	1666	Ancona
		1667	Naples
		1669	Ferrara
			Florence
		1670	Bologna
		1671	Roma
		1673	Lucca
1665	*Muzio Scevola*	1665	Bologna

APPENDIX II

Cavalli's extant sacred music

'Cantate Domino' in Ghirlanda Sacra (ed. Simonetti), 1625
'O quam suavis' in *Motetti a voce sola di diversi Eccelentissimi Autori,* 1645
Magnificat, in *Messa a 4 voci, et salmi* by Monteverdi (ed. Cavalli), 1650

'In virtute tua'	in *La Sacra Corona* (ed. Marcesso). 1656. The
'O bone Jesu'	latter two pieces were reprinted in *Sacri*
'Plaudite, cantate'	*Concerti* (ed. Silvani), Bologna, 1668

Musiche Sacre concernenti messa, e salmi concertati con istromenti, imni, antifone et sonate a due, 3, 4, 5, 6, 8, 10 e 12 voci (Venice, 1656), containing:

Messa
'Dixit Dominus'
'Confitebor tibi Domine'
'Beatus vir'
'Laudate pueri'
'Laudate Dominum'
'Laetatus sum'
'Nisi Dominus'
'Lauda Jerusalem'
Credidi'
'In convertendo'
'Domine probasti'
'Iste confessor'
'Ave maris stella'
'Jesu corona virginum'
'Exultet orbis'
'Deus tuorum militum'
Magnificat
'Ave regina coelorum'
'Regina caeli'
'Salve regina'
'Alma redemptoris mater'
Canzoni/sonate a 3, 4, 6, 8, 10 and 12.

Vesperi a 8 voci (Venice, 1675), containing:

1. *Vespero della Beata Vergine*

'Dixit Dominus'
'Laudate pueri'

'Laetatus sum'
'Nisi Dominus'
'Lauda Jerusalem'
Magnificat

2. *Vespero delle Domeniche, et altri Salmi (con li salmi correnti di tutto l'anno)*

'Dixit Dominus'
'Confitebor'
'Beatus vir'
'Laudate pueri'
'In exitu Israel'
'Laudate Dominum'
'Credidi'
'In convertendo'
'Domine probasti'
'Beati omnes'
'De profundis'
'Memento'
'Confitebor Angelorum'
Magnificat

3. *Vespero delle Cinque Laudate (ad uso della Capella di S. Marco)*

'Laudate pueri'
'Laudate Dominum omnes gentes'
'Laudate anima mea'
'Laudate Dominum quoniam bonus'
'Lauda Jerusalem'
Magnificat

Missa pro defunctis a 8 (Score in D-Bds, D1, according to Eitner; modern copy in Bnm)

APPENDIX III

Documentary extracts

i. ASV, Procuratori di S Marco, Procuratia de supra, fasc. 35; Decreti e terminazioni, reg. 141, f.53v.
ii. from *Madrigali Concertati . . . del Signor Gio: Rovetta . . . dedicati al . . . Sig. Francesco Cavalli* (Venice, Vincenti, 1645)
iii. from ASV, Notarile Claudio Paulini, Testamenti, b.799, f.381
iv. ASV, Scuola Grande di S Marco, b.188, f.14.
v. *Musiche Sacre . . . di Francesco Cavalli* (Venice, Vincenti, 1656)
vi. Paris, BN, Ministère des Affaires Etrangères, *Rome* 137, f.263.
vii. ASV, Procuratori di S Marco, Procuratia de supra, fasc.35; Decreti e terminazioni, reg.146, f.75v.
viii. ASV, Scuola Grande di S Marco, b.188, f.380.

i. Che siano condutti per cantori in chiesa di S Marco l'infrascritti soprani, uno di quale Eunuche, quali sono stati sentiti da SS. SS. Ecc. me at anco havutta relaz. e dal Maestro di Cappella, che sono a proposito il servizio della Chiesa con salario di ducati ottanta per cadauno, et a bene plauso di SS. SS. III.mi.
  Piero Franco Bruni, cremasco
  Felice Cazzelari, da Pistoia eununco

ii. Sono questi però scherzi della penna del Signor Gio: Rovetta mio zio materno, tanto partial ammiratore del merito di V.S. Onde havro fatto in questo affare a fidanza col Zio, per mostrar la mia devota riverenza ad un Padrone; honorando le fatiche dell'uno con la protezzione delll'altro, che si è tanto affaticato nell'indrizzarmi per quella via, nella quale egli s'è condotto già al sommo della virtù.

L'Organo di S Marco reso divino dalla dotta mano di V.S. è la minor prova, ch'ella fà del suo molto valore.

Posciache l'esquisitezza delle sue celebratissime compositioni è tale, ch'ella rapisce con esse loro e nelle Chiese, e nelle Camere, e ne' Teatri gli animi di tutti.

Ritenuta però V.S. và tanto in publicarle al mondo, che defrauda con la sua troppa modestia l'ansioso desiderio della commune curiosa richiesta.

E veramente mentre concorrono in lei trè qualità esimie, ch'ella, e sà vestire nobilmente i soggetti, e impareggiabilmente cantarli, e accompagnarli con la leggiadra accuratezza sù l'istromento, credo io che non voglia V.S. far torto con metter alla stampa le sue ottime compositione, allaltre due prerogative ch'ella possiede, di ben cantarle e accompagnarle, che sono vivi tesori incapaci della stampa.

iii. . . . Protestando che si io lascio ogni cosa al sudetto mio consorte, gli lascio più del suo, che del mio, havendo lui nel tempo che siamo stati insieme mantenuto, et spesato tutti li mieie, cioè Madre, Fratello, sorella, Ameda, figlioli et tutto il mio parentado, hora l'uno, hora l'altro secondo l'occasioni, et il bisogno, di modo che è per volontà, et per conscienza ancora devo lasciarlo assoluto patrone di tutto il mio si come con tutto il Core faccio . . .

iv. Benche V.S. Ecc.ma vegga l'affetto c'hò sempre portato à lei, al suo Teatro, e riverenza insieme à gli Ill.mi interessati; Le fò sapere, come io ultimamente mi abboccai coll' Ill.mo Duodo; e frà le cose concertate assieme per frase nella scritt.ra furono q.te.

Che non si parlasse di far suonare quel 3.o stromento, bastando solo la mia esibitione in Voce.

Che fatta la p.a. R.ta mi fosse datto scudi d'Arg. to 100.

Che ogni 4 R.te mi fossero datti D.ti 50 fino all'intero sodisf.ne delli D.to 400.

Queste cose mi furno cortesissimam.te promessa da d.to S.re ma uon attese poi nella scritt.ra ch'in vece di prove (come l'appuntato) li scudi 100 la p.a sera gli hà posti doppo la 3.a sera. Li D.ti 50 in cambio delle 4 gli hà posti doppo le sei; onde io vedendo che non mi si mantenava in scritto, quel tanto ch'in voce mi s'era promesso, regolai d.ta scritt.a, e si come esso Ill.mo Duodo mà l'havea mandata à me; Io la rimandai à esso S.re corretta in questa forma, a ciò fosse sotto scritta, et ultimamente q.to neg.o, incominciato fù questa quadrag.ma. Veggo però dalle longhezze di questo neg.o et delle dilationi nel concludere, la poca stima che si fà della mia persona, che perciò un Mese fà mi licentiai (con una mia) dall' Ill.mo Duodo, mà per portar me la anco più à longo non vuolse accettarla, onde per venirne à un fine, scrivo questa à lei che servirà per tutta la Compag.a e per informatione che se per tutto Dimani, che sara li 24 che e Lunedi non mi haveranno rissolto con la sotto scrittione alla scritt.a inviata, io mi dichiaro libero del trattato fin hora havuto insieme.

V.S. Ecc.ma non havrà occ.ne di dolersi di me, mentre stà à loro S.ri l'havermi; dichiarandomi pronto a servirli, mentre mi sij sottoscritta la d.ta scritt.a, che non è stravagante, ma è conforme il concerto pred.to: ne è variata in altro (nella forma del pagamento) che di due sere più, meno, dell'esborso delli 100 scudi et di una sera di meno, di questo delli D.ti 50 cosa che non sò credere che sij Cagione di non mi contentare con una sodisf.ne di si poco momento. Servà però come ho d.to questa per avviso, che s'io non riceverò questa sotto scritt.ne per utto Mercordi come sopra, m'intenderò d'ogni oblig.ne con loro S.i. e le bacio la mano.

v. Il mio Genio è stato sempre lontano dalle stampe; e hò più tosto aconsentito à lasciar correre le mie debolezze dove le portò la fortune col mezo della penna, che con quello de Torchi. Al fine però mi sono lasciato persuader dalle instanze del Signor Alessandro Vincenti, che, doppo lunga persistenza nella mia opinione hà saputo vincermi, e darmi ardire di esponere all'universo i deboli tratte delle mie Note. Se tu riceverai gradimento siane egli il benemerito; come pure, se ne incontri tedio non dolerti di me, che à recarti questo incommodo per altro fine non mi sono condotto, solo che per compiacere in amico, che con le sue cortesie hà saputo persuadermi.

Osserverai, che frà le Parti Alto, Tenore e Basso del secondo Choro hò inserite le Sinfonie per tre tromboni, ò simili stromenti; le quali cosi hò poste per non moltiplicare in libri separati: avverti però, che quelli si possono anco tralasciare ad arbitrio; mà nel tempo di quelle doveranno tacere le Parti che Cantano, come se in luoco di dette Sinfonie fossero notate le Pause: In oltre le detti Tromboni, ò altri stromenti, che fossero, doveranno suonare per tutto dove si troverà la parola TUTTI, e cessare dove sarà la parola SOLI. Et in questo stesso modo si possono adoperare qualunque altre parti per far maggiori ripieni, sempre ciò facendo ottima riuscita.

Di più avverti, che la Parte del Violoncino (la quale starà bene appresso li violini, gareggiando quella insieme con essi) si può adoperare, e tralasciare à piacimento. Nel resto compatisci, e vivi lungamente felice.

vi. Non ha modi la mia penna che siano sufficienti per esprimere quali siano i sentimenti della riverenza con la quale registro nel cuore la benignità, con che cotesto Ecc.mo S.r Cardinale Mazarino inclina alle mie glorie et a sublimarmi alla felicità di servire a si gran Corona; et in oltre mi conosco inhabile a i dovuti rendim.ti di gratie verso di V.S. Ill.ma che si di cuore intraprende il persuadermi a venire ad incontrar tanta Fortuna. Può sicuro credere S. Em. che l'anima conserverà verso il di lui augustissimo merito, con l'immortalità propria, immortale l'ossequio; e V.S. Ill.ma può assicurarsi di tutta la mia divotione per tutti i momenti del mio vivere. Creda V.S. Ill.ma che non l'eccitamento delle mille doble e d'altre offerte, ma la conoscenza che hò di quanto sia gloriosa la Fortuna, che mi s'incontrò, mi fecero piegare tutto il mio stato a venir costà; e creda come Evangelio, che dopo scritto, a migliori riflessi della mia età, della mia complessione, e del mio costume a quest'aria, ero pentito: tuttavia io non mi potevo all' hora rimovere. Il Cielo, che dirige per vie ignote il meglio, se bene noi non lo conosciamo, fece che l'essermi mancate le conditioni, che m'erano state promesse, non che queste che havevo richieste, mi diede modo di ritirarmi: et assicuro V.S. Ill.ma della mia fede, che non la diminutione delle promesse mi disviò, ma la conoscenza dell'havere una complessione impotente a questo viaggio et alla servitù che si doverebbe prestare, mi fece incontrare l'occasione, che bramavo, di ritirarmi da passi a' quali il desiderio di servire a si Gran Prencipi et a Re si famoso, m'haveva condotto, se bene l'inabilità mi doveva ritenere dal farli.

Io hò una complessione debolissima per natura, aggravata dall'età e dallo studio fatto, indi dallo escercitio. Compongo solo all'hora che me ne prende la fantasia, e sono si poco resistente alla fatica, che, se un hora di più del mio uso m'affatico, sono sunito amalato. Hor che V.S. Ill.ma consideri se sono da pormi a questo pericolo di viaggio e se potrò poi servire come doverei. In vero sarebbe un venire a comprarmi la morte. Quanto poi alle cose mie, dopo disciolti i passati trattati, li ho qui raffermati. Sono obligato a Cavalieri Grandi, ad impieghi utilissimi et a teatri, con stipendio rilevante, cose tutte che non mi giova abbandonarle, mentre che hò qui in casa comodi a mio talento, per andar incontro ad incomodi evidenti, a rischi diversi et a cimenti di perdere il tutto con me medesimo.

Di tutto quello ch'io possa di qui, S. Em. e Padrone e V.S. Ill.ma hora per sempre riceva la mia devozione, e, se ci disgiongono i Regni, si assicuri che mi legano ad esser costà con l'essequio, le obligationi che devo alla stima che conosco farsi della mia debolezza. Consacro a S. Em. la mia penna, mentre non posso a piedi inchinarmi con lo individuo e tutto ciò ch'io vaglia havrò sempre debito corrisponderlo ad ogni suo cenno, e se costà non posso venire, mando il cuore humiliato, e l'anima riverente che in eterno sarà schiava di S. Em. e mi conserverà sempre.

vii. Sia concesso à Domino Francesco Cavalli organista che parta per Francia quando sarà da detto Sig. Ambasciatore ricercato per le solennità del matrimonio del Re Crist.mo, et ivi si tratengo fino al fine di dette solennità, con sicurezza, che gli sarà riservato il luoco ed emolumento suo fino al suo ritorno in questa Città: cosi essendo anco la pubblica intentione dell'Ecc.mo Senato. Dovendo trà tanto impiegarti nella funtione d'organista in luogo di detto Cavali Don Gio: Batt.a Volpe come egli stesso si è offerito senza altra mercede, che di acquistar merito col ben servire.

viii. [Se] bene io sò dal lEcc.mo Minato Ella havrà inteso . . . le mie ragioni circa il servirla il prossimo carnevale . . . non voglio però restare di attestarle anch'io con . . . i miei sentimenti, accio non incolpasse mai il mio . . . circa la persona sua e l'antica mia servitù. . . . ritornato di Francia con fermissimo proponimento [di non] affaticarmi più in opere teatrali. Alle sue instanze . . . a quelle (à nome suo) fattemi dall'Ecc.mo Minato non hò potuto resistere, onde ho condisceso à compiacerla a servirla, col . . . in musica l'opera si come hò sempre fatto, sebene havevo stabilito di non prendere più questo impaccio; mà à questa affettuosa risolutione mi s'interpone un intoppo, posto però da . . . e non da me; perche Ella vorrebbe due opere, et io per il poco tempo non posso prometterglile, havendo anco altri miei interessi proprii, che mi tengono occupato.

Io hò tradito la mia voluntà per renderla servita; Lei stà ferma, è salda in voler compiacere in tutto a se stessa. Gli hò fatto essibire per secondo l'opera reggia, fatta in Francia, stimando che fosse per aggradirla volontieri si come sono sicurissimo che tutta la città concorrerebbe curiosa à vederla e sentirla; ma di questo ne anco s'appaga; crede à mè, si chiude la strada di effettuare con le operationi la brama che hò di poterla servire. . . . per anto V.S. Ecc.ma della mia buona volonta. . . . la mia ostinatione, mentre hò condisceso (come . . .) che posso; e s'assicuri, che se il tempo me lo permetesse . . . [non] risparmierei fattica anco d'avvantaggio . . . in tutto, e devotamente le baccio le mani.

APPENDIX IV

Modern editions

1. OPERA

L'Ormindo, ed. R. Leppard (London, 1969)
La Calisto, ed. R. Leppard (London, 1975)
L'Eritrea, ed. J. Glover (London, 1977)

2. SACRED MUSIC

'Cantate Domino', ed. F. Vatielli in *Antiche cantate spirituali* (Turin, 1922)
MESSA (1656), ed. R. Leppard (London, 1966)
'Laudate Dominium', ed. R. Leppard (London, 1966)
'Laetatus sum', ed. R. Leppard (London, 1969)
Magnificat (1656), ed. R. Leppard (London, 1973)
'Ave regina caelorum', ed. B. Stäblein in *Musica divina* i (Regensburg, 1950)
'Regina caeli', ed. B. Stäblein in *Musica divina* ii (Regensburg, 1950)
'Salve regina', ed. B. Stäblein in *Musica divina* iii (Regensburg, 1950); also ed. R. Leppard (London, 1969)
'Alma redemptoris mater', ed. B. Stäblein in *Musica divinia* iv (Regensburg, 1950)
3 Magnificats from *Vesperi a 8* (1675), ed. G. Piccioli (Milan, 1960)

Bibliography

List of abbreviations

AM	:	Acta Musicologica
Grove 6	:	Grove's Dictionary of Music and Musicians (forthcoming issue)
JAMS	:	Journal of the American Musicological Society
JbP	:	Jahrbuch der Musikbibliothek Peters
MF	:	Die Musikforschung
MfM	:	Monatshefte für Musik-Geschichte
MGG	:	Die Musik in Geschichte und Gegenwart
ML	:	Music and Letters
MM	:	Mercure Musical
MQ	:	Musical Quarterly
MR	:	Music Review
MT	:	Musical Times
NRMI	:	Nuova Rivista Musicale Italiana
PRMA	:	Proceedings of the Royal Musical Association
RassM	:	Rassegna Musicale
RID	:	Rivista Italiana di Dramma
RIM	:	Rivista Italiana di Musica
RM	:	Revue Musicale
RMI	:	Rivista Musicale Italiana
SImg	:	Sammelbande der Internationalen Musik-Gesellschaft
SMW	:	Studien zur Musikwissenschaft
VfM	:	Viertal jahrsschrift für Musikwissenschaft

ABERT, A.A., *Claudio Monteverdi und das Musikalisches Drama* (Lippstadt, 1945)
— 'Cavalli' in *MGG* II (Kassel and Basel, 1951), cc.926–932
— 'Aureli' in *MGG* I (1949–1951), cc.859–862
— 'Busenello' in *MGG* II (1951), cc.511–513
— 'Faustini' in *MGG* III (1954), cc.1881–1883
— 'Minato' in *MGG* IX (1961), cc.348–350

ADEMOLLO, Alessandro, *I primi fasti della musica italiana a Parigi 1645–1662* (Milan, 1884)

—*I teatri di Roma nel secolo decimosettimo* (Rome, 1888)

— *I primi fasti del Teatro di Via della Pergola in Firenze 1657–1661* (Milan, 1885)

AGAZZARI, Agostino, 'Del sonare sopra il basso' (1607) Translated in Strunk: *Source Readings in Music History*, pp.424–431.

ALDRICH, Putnam, 'The Authentic Performance of Baroque Music' in *Essays in Honor of A.T. Davison* (Cambridge, Mass., 1957), pp.161–171

—*Rhythm in Seventeenth Century Monody* (New York, 1966)

ALLACCI, Lione, *Drammaturgia . . . accresciuta e continuata fino all'anno 1755* (Venice, 1755. First published Rome, 1666)

AMBROS, A.W., 'Francesco Cavalli' in *Neue Zeitschrift für Musik* LXV (1869), p.313, pp.321–324

d'AMICO, S., *Storia del teatro drammatico* (Milan, 1958)

—*Epoche del teatro italiano* (Florence, 1954)

d'ANCONA, A., *Origini del teatro italiano* (Turin, 1891)

APOLLONIO, M., *Storia del teatro italiano* (Florence, 1950)

ARNOLD, Denis., *Monteverdi* (London, 1963)

— ' "L'Incoronazione di Poppea" and its orchestral requirements' in *MT* CIV (1963), pp.176–178

— 'Francesco Cavalli: some recently discovered documents' in *ML* (1965), p.50ff.

— 'Monteverdi; some colleagues and pupils' in *The Monteverdi Companion* (eds. D. Arnold and N. Fortune, London, 1968), pp.110–130

— 'Alessandro Grandi, a Disciple of Monteverdi' in *MQ* XLIII (1957), pp.171–186

— 'A background note on Monteverdi's hymn settings' in *Scritti in onore di Luigi Ronga* (Milan–Naples, 1973)

ARNOLD, Frank J., *The art of accompaniment from a thorough bass as practised in the seventeenth and eighteenth centuries* (London, 1931)

ARRIGONI, R. *Notizie ed osservazioni intorno all'origine e al progresso dei Teatri e delle rappresentazioni teatrale in Venezia e nelle città principali dei paesi Veneti* (Venice, 1840)

ARTEAGA, Stefano, *Le rivoluzioni del teatro musicale italiano dalla sua origine fino al presente* (Venice, 1785)

BARBLAN, Guglielmo, *Claudio Monteverdi* (Turin, 1967)

— 'Venezia e Roma sono le uniche scuole del barocco musico italiano?' in *Festschrift Heinrich Besseler zum sechzigsten Geburtstag* (Leipzig, 1961), pp.285–289.

— 'Il termine "barocco" e la musica' in *Miscellanea en homenaje a Monseñor Higinio Angeles* (Barcelona, 1958–1961), pp.93–108.

BATTAGLIA, Michele, *Saggio storico della Nobiltà Patrizia Veneta* (Venice, 1816)

—*Delle Accademie Veneziane* (Venice, 1826)

BEAT, Janet E., 'Monteverdi and the Opera Orchestra of his time' in *The Monteverdi Companion* (eds. D. Arnold and N. Fortune, London, 1968), pp.277–301

BELLONI, A., *Il Seicento* (Milan, 1929)

BENVENUTI, Giacomo, 'Il manoscritto veneziano della "Incoronazione di Poppea" ' in *RMI* XLI (1937), pp.176–184.

BETTINELLI, Giuseppe, *Famiglie patrizie venete . . . Il tutto ristrettamente cavato da una cronaca manuscritta in quattro volumi . . . essistente nella Pubblica Libreria di Venezia* (Venice, 1774)

BIANCONI, Lorenzo, 'Caletti (Caletti-Bruni), Pietro Francesco, detto Cavalli' in *Dizionario Biografico degli Italiani* XVI (1973), pp.686–696.

— *Francesco Cavalli und die Verbreitung der venezianischen Oper in Italien* (dissertation, University of Heidelberg, 1974)

— ' "L'Ercole in Rialto" ' in *Venezia e il melodramma nel seicento* (ed. M.T. Muraro, Florence, 1976), pp.259–272

BIANCONI, Lorenzo and WALKER, Thomas, 'Dalla *Finta Pazza* alla *Veremonda;* storie di Febiharmonici' in *RIM* X (1975), pp.379–454.

BJURSTROM, P., *Giacomo Torelli and Baroque Stage Design* (Stockholm, 1961)

BLUME, Friedrich, *Renaissance and Baroque Music* (Norton, 1967)

BOERIO, *Dizionario del dialetto veneziano* (Venice, 1827; second edition 1856)

BONAVENTURA, A., *Saggio storico sul teatro musicale italiano* (Leghorn, 1913)

BONLINI, Giovanni Carlo, *Le glorie della poesia e della musica contenute nell' esatta notizia de teatri dell Città di Venezia* (Venice, 1730)

BONTA, Stephen, 'The Uses of the Sonata da Chiesa' in *JAMS* XXII, 1 (1969), pp.54–84

BOYER, Ferdinand, 'Les Orsini et les Musiciens d'Italie au debut du XVIIe siècle' in *Mélanges de philologie d'histoire et de litterature offerts à Henri Haurette* (Paris, 1934), pp.301–310

BRATTI, Ricciotti, *I codici nobiliari del Museo Correr di Venezia* (Rome, 1908)

BRIZI, Bruno, 'Teoria e prassi melodrammatica di G.F. Busenello e 'L'Incoronazione di Poppea" ' in *Venezia e il melodramma nel seicento* (ed. M.T. Muraro, Florence, 1976), pp.51–74.

BRUNELLI, Bruno, 'L'impresario in angustie' in *RID* III (1941), pp.311–341

BUKOFZER, Manfred, *Music in the Baroque Era* (London, 1948)

BURNEY, Charles, *A General History of Music* (London, 1789)

BUSSI, F., *La messa concertata et la musique sacrée de Pier Francesco Cavalli* (Paris, 1960)

— 'La produzione sacra di Cavalli e i suoi rapporti con quella di

Monteverdi' in *RIM* II (1967), pp.229–254

CAFFI, Francesco, *Storia della musica Teatrale in Venezia* Unpublished work in five manuscript boxes: Bnm IV.747 (=10462–6)

——*Storia della Musica Sacra nella già Cappella Ducale di San Marco in Venezia 1318–1797* (Venice, 1854; reprinted Milan, 1931)

CAMERINI, Paolo, *Piazzola* (Milan, 1925)

CAMETTI, A., *Il teatro di Tordinona poi d'Apollo* (Tivoli, 1938)

CANAL, Pietro, *Della Musica in Mantova* (Venice, 1881)

CANEVAZZI, G., *Papa Clemente IX poeta* (Modena, 1900)

CAPRI, A., *Il melodramma dalle origine ai nostri giorni* (Modena, 1938)

CARINI MOTTA, Fabrizio, *Trattato sopra la struttura de' Teatri e scene* (1676: edited E. Craig, Azzate, 1972)

CARRICK, Edward, 'Theatre Machines in Italy 1400–1800' in *The Architectural Review* LXX (1931), p.2ff

CASTIGLION, Niccola, 'Significato storico del melodramma nella prima metà del seicento' in *RassM* XXV (1956), pp.196–203

CECCHITI, Bartolomeo, 'Carte relativo ai teatri di S. Cassiano e dei Santi Giovanni e Paolo' in *Archivio Veneto* XVII (1887), p.246 ff

CHAMBERS, D.S., *The Imperial Age of Venice 1380–1580* (London, 1970)

CHIARELLI, Alessandra, '"L'Incoronazione de Poppea" ò 'Il Nerone': problemi di filologia testuale' in *RIM* IX (1974), pp.117–151

CICOGNA, E.A., *Illustri muranesi richiamati alla memoria* (Venice, 1858)

—— *Saggio di Bibliografia Veneziana* (Venice, 1847)

CLEMENT, F. and LAROUSSE, P., *Dictionnaire lyrique, ou Histoire des Opéras* (Paris, 1905)

della CORTE, Andrea, *Dramma per musica dal Rinuccini allo Zeno* (Turin, 1958)

— 'Tragico e comico nell'opera veneziana della seconda parte del seicento' in *RassM* XI (1938), pp.325–333

CORYAT, Thomas, *Coryat's Crudities* (Glasgow, 1905)

CRAIG, E.G., 'John Evelyn and the theatre in England, France and Italy' in *The Mask* (1924)

CRAIN, G.F., 'Francesco Cavalli and the Venetian Opera' in *Opera* XVIII (1967), pp.446–451

CROCE, Benedetto, *I teatri di Napoli dal Rinascimento alla fine del secolo decimottavo* (Bari, 1966)

DENT, E.J., 'A Jesuit at the Opera in 1680' in *Riemann-Festschrift* (Leipzig, 1909), pp.381–393

DIZIONARIO *delle favole per uso delle Scuole d'Italia . . . e i di cui soggetti sono cavati dalla Storia Poetica* (Venice, 1796)

DIZIONARIO *storico-partabile di tutte le venete patrizie famiglie* (Venice, 1780)

DOGLIONI, N., *Le cose notabile et maravigliose della città di Venezia* (Venice, 1655, under pseudonym L. Goldioni; reprinted 1671)

DONI, G.B., 'Discorso sopra la Perfettione delle Melodie ò de' Concenti' in *Compendio del trattato de' generi e de' modi della Musica* (Rome, 1635), pp.95–125

DONINGTON, Robert, *The Interpretation of Early Music* (New York, 1963; reprinted London, 1974)

DUCHARTRE, Pierre L., *The Italian Comedy* (translated by R.T. Weaver; London, 1929)

EITNER, Robert, *Bibliographisch-Bibliographisches quellen-Lexicon II* (Leipzig, 1900–1904)

—— *Die Oper von ihren ersten Anfängen bis zur Mitte des 18 Jahrhunderts II* (Berlin, 1883)

EVELYN, John, *Diary* (ed. E.S. de Beer, Oxford, 1955)

FASSINI, Sesto, *Teatro del Seicento* (Milan–Naples, 1956)

FORTI, Delfina, 'I drammi pastorale del '600' in *Ateneo Veneto,* 1903

FORTUNE, Nigel, 'Italian secular monody from 1600 to 1625: An Introductory Survey' in *MQ* (1953), pp.171–195

—— 'Italian seventeenth-century singing in *ML* (1954), pp.206–219

FRANCO, Giacomo, *Habiti d'huomini e donne venetiani* (Venice, 1610)

FURTTENBACH, Joseph, *Architectura recreationis* (Augsburg, 1640)

GALVANI, Livio, *I Teatri Musicali di Venezia nel secolo XVII* (Milan, 1878)

GIAZZOTTO, Remo, 'La guerra dei palchi' in *NRMI* 1967, pp.245–268; 465–508

—— *Il melodramma a Genova nei secoli XVII e XVIII* (Genoa, 1941)

GLOVER, Jane, *The Teatro Sant' Apollinare and the development of seventeenth-century Venetian opera* (D.Phil. thesis, Oxford, 1975)

—— 'Cavalli and Rosinda' in *MT* CXIV (1973), pp.133–135

—— 'Aria and closed form in the operas of Francesco Cavalli' in *The Consort* XXXII (1976), pp.167–175

GOLDSCHMIDT, Hugo, *Studien zu Geschichte der italien Oper im 17. Jahrhundert, I* (Leipzig, 1901)

—— 'Cavalli als dramatischer Komponist' in *MfM* XXV (1893), pp.45–48, 53–57, 61–111

—— 'Das instrumentalbegleitung der Italienischen Musikdrama in der ersten Halfte des XVII Jahrhunderts' in *MfM* XXVIII (1895), pp.52–62

—— 'Das orchester der italienischen Oper in 17. Jahrhunderts' in *SImg* II (1900–1901), pp.16–75

GROPPO, Antonio, *Notizia generale de' teatri della città di Venezia* (Venice, 1766)

— *Catalogo di tutti drammi per musica recitati ne' teatri di Venezia dall'anno 1637 all'anno presente 1745* (Venice, 1745)

GROUT, Donald J., *A Short History of Opera* (Oxford, 1947; Columbia, 1964)

— 'The Chorus in early opera' in *Festschrift Friedrich Blume zum 70 Geburtstag* (ed. Abert, Kassel, 1963)

GURLITT, W., 'Ein Briefwechsel zwichen Paul Hainlein und L. Friedrich Behaim aus den Jahren 1647–1648' in *SImg* XIV (1912–1913), p.491 ff

HAAS, R., *Die Musik des Barocks* (Potsdam, 1928)

HERIOT, A., *The Castrati in Opera* (London, 1956)

HEUSS, Alfred, 'Die Venetianischen Opern–Sinfonien' in *SImg* IV (1902–3), pp.404–477

HICKS, Anthony, 'Cavalli and *La Calisto*' in *MT* CXI (1970), pp.486–9

HITCHCOCK, H. Wiley, 'Vocal ornamentation in Caccinis *Nuove Musiche*' in *MQ* LVI (1970), pp.389–404

HJELMBORG, Bjorn, 'Une partition de Cavalli. (Quelques remarques complementaires aux recherches Cavalliennes)' in *AM* XVI–XVII (1944–45), pp.39–54

— 'Aspects of the aria in the early operas of Cavalli' in *Natalica Musicologica Knud Jeppeson* (Hafniae, 1962), pp.173–198

IVANOVICH, Cristoforo, *Minerva al tavolino* (Venice, 1681, 1688)

JANNACO, C., *Il seicento* (Milan, 1963)

KERMAN, Joseph, *Opera as Drama* (New York, 1956)

KRETSCHMAR, Hermann, 'Beitrage zur Geschichte der venetianischen Oper' in *JbP* XIV (1907), pp.71–81

— *Geschichte d. Oper* (Leipzig, 1919)

— 'Die Venetianische Oper und die Werke Cavallis und Cestis' in *VfM* VIII (1892), pp.1–76

LEPPARD, Raymond, 'Cavalli's operas' in *PRMA* XCIII (1967), pp.67–76

— 'Unexplored relationships between early seventeenth-century Venetian opera and contemporary music in France and England' in *Proceedings of the British Academy,* LV (1971)

LIBRO *dei Nobili Veneti; ora per la prima volta messo in luce* (Florence, 1866)

LIVINGSTON, Arthur, *La vita veneziana nelle opere di Francesco Busenello* (Venice, 1913)

LOEWENBERG, A., *Annals of Opera, 1597–1940* (Cambridge, 1943)

LOGAN, Oliver, *Culture and Society in Venice, 1470–1790* (London, 1972)

MALIPIERO, G. Francesco, *Claudio Monteverdi* (Milan, 1930)
MANGINI, Nicola, *I teatri di Venezia* (Milan, 1974)
MARCHESI, G., *Per la storia della novella italiana nel secolo 17* (Rome, 1897)
MATTHESON, J. *Grundlage einer Ehren-Pforte* (Hamburg, 1740)
MAYLENDER, M., *Storia delle Accademie d'Italia* (Bologna, 1926)
MOLMENTI, P.G., *La storia di Venezia nella vita privata dalle origini alla caduta della republica* (Bergamo, 1905–8)
MONDOLFO BOSSARELLI, A., 'Ancora intorno al codice napoletano della 'Incoronazione di Poppea' in *RIM* II (1967), p.294 ff
MORELLI, Giovanni and WALKER, Thomas, 'Tre controversie intorno al S Cassiano' in *Venezia e il melodramma nel seicento* (ed. M.T. Muraro, Florence, 1976)
da MOSTO, Andrea, *L'Archivio di Stato in Venezia* (Rome, 1939)
—— *Il teatro a Venezia nel secolo XVII* (Rome, 1899)
MURARO, Maria Theresa, 'Venezia' in *Enciclopedia dello spettacolo* III (Rome, 1956), pp.268–71
MUTINI, Claudio, 'Aureli' in *Dizionario Biografico degli Italiani* IV (1962), pp.587–8

OREGLIA, Giacomo, *The Commedia dell'arte* (London, 1970)
ORLOFF, G., *Essai sur l'histoire de la musique* (Paris, 1822)
OROLOGIO *del piacere che mostra l'ore del dilettevole soggiorno hauto dall'altezza serenissima d'Ernest Augusto Vesovo d'Osnabruc, Duca di Branswich, Lunebergo etc.* (Piazzola, 1685)
OSTHOFF, Wolfgang, 'Neue Beobachtungen zu Quellen und Geschichte von Monteverdis "'Incoronazione di Poppea'" in *MF* XI (1958), pp.129–138
—— 'Zur Bologneser Anffuhrung von Monteverdis "Ulisse" in Jahr 1640' in *Oesterreichische Akademie der Wissenschaft i Anzeiger der philosophisch-historischen Klasse* XCV (1958), pp.155 ff
—— *Monteverdi-Studien I: Das dramatische Spätwerk Claudio Monteverdis* (Tutzing, 1960)
—— *Theatergesang und darstellende Musik in der italienischen Renaissance* (Tutzing, 1969)
—— 'Die venezianische und neapolitanische Fassung von Monteverdis "L'Incoronazione di Poppea" ' in *AM* XXVI (1954), pp.88–113
—— 'Antonio Cesti's "Alessandro, vincitor de si stesso" ' in *SMW* XXIV (1960), pp.13–43
—— 'Maschera e musica' in *NRMI* I (1967), pp.16–44

PALISCA, Claude V., 'Girolamo Mei: Mentor to the Florentine Camerata' in *MQ* XL (1954), pp.1–20
—— *Girolamo Mei: Letters on Ancient and Modern Music to Vincenzo Galilei and*

Giovanni Bardi (Rome, 1960)
—*Baroque Music* (New Jersey, 1968)
— 'The Alterati of Florence: pioneers in the theory of drama and music' in *New Looks at Italian Opera (Essays in Honor of D.J. Grout)* (ed. W. Austin, Ithaca, 1968)
— 'The "Camerata fiorentina": a Reappraisal' in *Studi musicali* I (1972), pp.203–236
PELLEGRINI, A., *Spettacoli lucchesi nei secc. XVII–XIX* I (Lucca, 1914)
PENNA, Lorenzo, *Li primi albori musicali* (Bologna, 1672)
PETROBELLI, Pierluigi, ' "L'Ermiona" di Pio Enea degli Obizzi ed i primi spettacoli d'opera veneziani' in *Quaderni della Rassegna musicale* III (1965), p.128 ff
— 'Francesco Manelli—documenti e osservazioni' in *Chigiana* XXIV (Nuova Serie, 4) (1967), pp.43–66
PIRROTTA, Nino, 'Early opera and aria' in *New Looks at Italian Opera (Essays in Honor of D.J. Grout)* (ed. W. Austin, Ithaca, 1968), pp.39–107
— 'Temperaments and tendencies in the Florentine Camerata' in *MQ* XL (1954), pp.169–189
— 'Tre capitoli su Cesti' in *La Scuola Romana* (Siena, 1953), pp.27–80
— 'Le prime opere di A. Cesti' in *L'Orchestra* (Florence, 1954), pp.154–177
— 'Il caval zoppo e il vetturino. Cronache di Parnasso, 1642' in *Collectanea historia musicae* IV (1966), pp.215–226
— 'Cavalli' in *Enciclopedia dello spettacolo* III (Rome, 1956), pp.268–271
—*Li due Orfei da Poliziano e Monteverdi* (Turin, 1969)
— 'Commedia dell'arte e opera' in *MQ* XLI (1955), pp.305–324
POWERS, Harold S., 'L'Erismena travestita' in *Studies in Music History* (ed. H.S. Powers, Princeton, 1968), pp.259–324
— 'Il Serse trasformato' in *MQ* XLVII (1961), pp.481–492
— 'Il Mutio tramutato: sources and libretto' in *Venezia e il melodramma nel seicento* (ed. M.T. Muraro, Florence, 1976), pp.227–258
PRUNIERES, Henri, *Cavalli et l'opéra venetien au dix-septième siècle* (Paris, 1931)
—*L'Opéra italien en France avant Lulli* (Paris, 1913)
— 'Les opéras de Francesco Cavalli' in *RM* XII (1931), pp.1–16, 125–147
— 'I libretti dell'opera veneziana nel Seicento' in *RassM* III (1930), pp.441–448
— 'Notes sur une partition faussement attribuée à Cavalli: L'Eritrea (1686)' in *RMI* XXVII (1920), pp. 267–273

REINER, Stuart, 'Vi sono molt'altre mezz'arie' in *Studies in Music History* (ed. H.S. Powers, Princeton, 1968)
— 'Collaboration in "Chi soffre sprei" ' in *MR* XXII (1961), pp.265–282
RICCI, Conrado, *I teatri di Bologna nei secoli XVII e XVIII* (Bologna, 1888)

ROBINSON, M.F., *Opera before Mozart* (London, 1966)
ROLANDI, Ulderigo, 'Le opere teatrali di Francesco Cavalli' in *Accademia musicale chigiana: La scuola veneziana* (1941)
—— *I libretti per musica attraverso i tempi* (Rome, 1951)
ROLLAND, Romain, 'Notes sur "L'Orfeo" de Luigi Rossi et sur les musiciens à Paris sous Mazarin' in *Congrès international d'histoire de la musique* (Paris, 1900)
—— *Histoire de l'opéra en Europe avant Lully et Scarlatti* (Paris, 1931)
—— 'L'Opéra populaire à Venise: Francesco Cavalli' in *MM* II (1906), pp.61–70, 151–160
—— *Les origines du théatre moderne: Histoire de l'opéra en Europe* (Paris, 1895)
ROMANIN, S., *Storia documentata di Venezia* (Venice, 1856)
ROSAND, Ellen, *Aria in the early operas of Francesco Cavalli* (Ph.D. dissertation. New York University, 1971)
—— 'Aria as drama in the early operas of Francesco Cavalli' in *Venezia e il melodramma nel seicento* (ed. M.T. Muraro, Florence, 1976), pp.75–96
—— 'L'Ormindo travestito in Erismena' in *JAMS* XXVIII (1975), pp.268–291
—— 'Comic contrast and dramatic unity: Observations on the form and function of aria in the operas of Francesco Cavalli' in *MR* XXXVII (1976), pp.92–105
—— 'Minato' in *Grove 6* (forthcoming)
ROSE, Gloria, 'Agazzari and the improvising orchestra' in *JAMS* XVIII (1965), pp.382–393
ROSE, P.L. 'The Accademia Venetiana: Science and Culture in Renaissance Venice' in *Studi veneziani* XI (1969), pp.191–242
ROWDON, Maurice, *The Fall of Venice* (London, 1970)

SABBATTINI, Nicola, *Pratica di fabricar scene e machine ne teatri* (Ravenna, 1638; ed. E. Povoledo, Rome, 1955)
SAINTDIDIER, Limojen de, *La ville et la République de Venise* (Paris, 1680)
SALZER, E.C., 'Teatro italiano in Vienna barocca' in *RID* I (1938), p.47 ff
SANSOVINO, F., *Venetia, città nobilissima* (Venice, 1581; second edition 1663, revised Martinioni)
SARTORI, Claudio, 'La prima diva della lirica italiana: Anna Renzi' in *NRMI* II (1968), pp.430–452
SCHEIBE, J.A., *Critischer Musikus* (Leipzig, 1745)
SCHNOEBELEN, Anna, 'Performance practices at San Petronio in the Baroque' in *AM* XLI (1969), pp.37–55
SCHOLZ, J., *Baroque and Romantic stage Design* (New York, 1962)
SCHRADE, Leo, *Monteverdi, Creator of Modern Music* (London, 1964)
SELFRIDGE-FIELD, Eleanor, *Venetian Instrumental Music from Gabrieli to Vivaldi* (Oxford, 1975)

SKIPPON, Sir Philip, *Journey through the Low Countries, Germany, Italy and France* (London, 1682; republished 1752)
SMITH, Patrick J., *The Tenth Muse: A historical study of the opera libretto* (London, 1971)
SOLERTI, Angelo, *Le origini del melodramma (Testimonianze dei Contemporanei)* (Turin, 1903)
— 'Lettere inedite sulla musica di Pietro della Valle a G.B. Doni ed una veglia drammatica-musicale del medesimo' in *RMI* XII (1905), pp.271–338
— *Gli albori del melodramma* (Milan, 1904–5)
— 'La Rappresentazione musicale di Venezia dal 1571 al 1605 per la prima volta descritta' in *RMI* IX (1902) pp.503–558
SONNECK, O. *Catalogue of Opera Librettos printed before 1800* (Washington, 1908, 1914)
SWALE, David, 'Cavalli: the "Erismena" of 1655' (in fact, 1671) in *Miscellanea Musicologica, Adelaide Studies in Musicology* III (1968), pp.145–170

TESTI, Flavio, *La musica italiana nel seicento* (Milan, 1970, 1972)
TORCHI, L., 'Canzoni ed Arie ad una voce nel seicento' in *RMI* I (1894)
— 'L'accompagnamento degli istrumenti nei melodrammi italiani della prima metà del seicento' in *RIM* I (1894), pp. 7–38; *RIM* II (1895), pp.666–671
TORELLI, L., *Il teatro italiano dalle origini ai nostri giorni* (Milan, 1924)
TOWNELEY WORSTHORNE, Simon, *Venetian Opera in the Seventeenth Century* (Oxford, 1954)
— 'Venetian theatres, 1637–1700' in *ML* XXIX (1948), pp.263–275
— 'Some early Venetian opera productions' in *ML* XXX (1949), pp.146–151

UBERTI, Enrico, *I Teatri di Venezia* (Venice, 1868)

VATIELLI, F., 'Operisti-librettisti dei secoli XVII e XVIII' in *RMI* XLIII (1939), pp.315–332
VETTER, Walther, 'Zur stil problematik des italienischen Oper des 17 und 18 Jahrunderts' in *Festschrift für Erich Schenk* (Graz, 1962), pp.561–573

WALKER, Thomas, See BIANCONI, L.
— See MORELLI, G.
— 'Gli errori di *Minerva al tavolino:* osservazioni sulla cronologia delle prime opere veneziane' in *Venezia e il melodramma nel seicento* (ed. M.T. Muraro, Florence, 1976), pp.7–20

—— 'Cavalli' in *Grove* 6 (forthcoming)
—— 'Busenello' in *Grove* 6 (forthcoming)
WEAVER, R.L., 'Orchestration in early Italian opera' in *JAMS* XVII (1964), p.83 ff.
—— 'Opera in Florence, 1646–1731' in *Studies in Musicology* (Chapel Hill, 1969), p.60 ff
WELLESZ, Egon, 'Cavalli und der Stil der venezianischen Oper von 1640–1660' in *SMW* I (1913), pp. 1–103
—— *Essays on Opera* (London, 1950)
—— 'De Aussetzung des basso continuo in der Italienische oper' in *International Music Society 4th Congress Report* (London, 1912), pp.282–285
WESTRUP, J.A., 'Monteverdi and the Orchestra' in *ML* XXI (1940), pp. 230–240
—— 'The Nature of Recitative' in *Proceedings of the British Academy* (London, 1956)
—— 'The Cadence in Baroque Recitative' in *Natalica musicologica Knud Jeppeson* (Hafniae, 1962), pp.243–252
WIEL, Taddeo, 'Francesco Cavalli e la sua musica scenica' in *Nuovo archivio veneto* XXVIII (Venice, 1914), p.142 ff
—— *I codici musicali Contariniani del secolo XVII nella R. Biblioteca di San Marco in Venezia* (Venice, 1888)
WOLEF, Hermann C., *Die venetianische Oper in der zweiten Hälfte des 17 Jahrhunderts* (Berlin, 1932)
—— 'Manierismus in den venezianischen Opernlibretti des 17 Jahrhunderts' in *Venezia e il melodramma nel seicento* (ed. M.T. Muraro, Florence, 1976), pp. 319–326
WOTQUENNE, Alfred, *Catalogue de la Bibliothéque du Conservatoire Royale de Bruxelles* (Brussels, 1901)
ZANON, Maffeo, *Venti arie tratte dei drami musicali di Francesco Cavalli* (Vienna-Trieste, 1909)

INDEX

Compiled by Frederick Smyth
Member of the Society of Indexers

The surnames of composers, referred to as such in the text, are printed in SMALL CAPITALS. Other professions or attributes are specified as necessary.

Page references in bold type denote extended mention of the subject. *bis* signifies that the subject can be found twice on the same page, and *ter* three times; *passim* (e.g., 50–6 *passim*) means that references are scattered throughout the pages; *n* and *nn* direct the reader to the Notes placed at the end of each chapter. q. stands for 'quoted' and q.v. for *quod vide* (which see).

(Ex.) or (Exx.) indicates that one or more musical examples from the work are included on the page(s).

S. Maria dei Carmini, Monastery of, 16
Sansovino, Francesco, author